The Five Principles of the Gospel

by C. Matthew McMahon

Copyright Information

Table of Contents

Introduction

When the Gospel is eclipsed, it is usually a result of misunderstanding the Gospel, and a negligence, of some sort, in preaching the word, (which is God's means of grace).[1] The word is silenced or hindered (possibly compromised), and so the *Gospel* is hindered (being understood merely from a human perspective). This seems obvious. But consider, God is *all powerful,*[2] yes, this is certainly true, however, God uses *means* to work out his decreed plan even though he is all powerful.[3] In other words, God can intervene directly (as with Old Testament or New Testament miracles), but generally he uses *means* in our day to accomplish his intended end (*i.e.* he uses the preached word). And when those means are not used according to God's prescription (when preachers are negligent in preaching, or are ignorant of the Bible), there is hindrance to spiritual growth in the church, and the Gospel becomes more or less eclipsed based on the poor use of those means. For example, if God says that his people should come to church and hear the preaching of the word, and they do not do this, then the means *of the preaching of the word* is not going to be helpful to them because they are abusing it by not

---

[1] ...as in the course of a world-wide pandemic where churches are closed all over world by order of the government.

[2] Gen. 17:1; Ruth 1:21; Job 13:3; Ezekiel 1:24; Rev. 11:7.

[3] "Thou shalt also decree a thing, and it shall be established unto thee: and the light shall shine upon thy ways," (Job 22:28).

attending it.[4] Though that may be a true sentiment, before one can deal adequately in exploring *that* idea, one must begin with, "what *is* the Gospel?" Before one can really talk about the Gospel itself *as a means*, the basic question of knowing *what the Gospel is* must come first. What are the principles of the Gospel that cannot be taken from Christ's Gospel and make the Gospel *not a Gospel?* That is a very important question to answer, *for one's faith and belief in the Gospel holds within it the eternal realities that cannot be undone after death.* To know the Gospel is to weigh eternity in the balance.

There are many Scriptures that people will use that they say *comprise* the Gospel. Let me give you just one that is, in the history of the Christian church, the most popular verse used to summarize the Gospel. "For God so loved the world, that he gave his only begotten Son, that whosoever believeth in him should not perish, but have everlasting life," (John 3:16). This is an excellent summary of the good news. Thomas Manton, Westminster Divine, agrees on this point. "In these words you have the sum and substance of the gospel."[5] This is excellent news! I agree with Manton, but, I have some questions to ask about this.

---

[4] Consider the horrible consequence of government policies in telling churches that they cannot worship because of the coronavirus.

[5] Manton, Thomas, *The Complete Works of Thomas Manton, D.D.* With memoir of the author by William Harris. Ed. T Smith, Volume 2, (London: J. Nisbet, 1870-75; reprinted., Worthington, PA: Maranatha Publications, 1980) 340.

It is interesting to note, that when Jesus sent out his disciples to preach *the Gospel,* he told them the following, "And as ye go, preach, saying, The kingdom of heaven is at hand," (Matt. 10:7). It is not my intention here, in this work, to discuss the differences between John 3:16 and Matthew 10:7. However, it is interesting to note, though, that John the Baptist,[6] Jesus Christ,[7] and his disciples preached *the kingdom* as the Gospel[8] (whatever *that* means) when they preached. And it is equally interesting to note that when they preached the message of the Great King and his salvation, they preached *the kingdom of God.*[9]

Aside from that "interesting notation" consider the substance of John 3:16. The verse is no doubt, an excellent verse. In fact, John 3:16 is my favorite verse in Scripture.[10] But when we ask the question, *what is the Gospel?* then answering *that* in light of a single verse like this one, or a summary verse like, "repent, for the Kingdom of Heaven is upon you," such verses hold various ideas in them where those who hear the preaching of the word have to *fill in.* What do I mean when I say this? When I say that the Gospel is certainly found in John 3:16, that is because I personally fill up John 3:16 with meaning that I know to be true because I

---

[6] Matthew 3:2.
[7] Matthew 4:17.
[8] Luke 9:2.
[9] See my work, *The Kingdom of Heaven is Upon You,* for a study of the Kingdom in this light.
[10] See my work, titled, *John 3:16,* Second Edition, at Puritan Publications.

have read the whole bible and understand some of the nuances of what Jesus is saying to Nicodemus in that John 3 passage. I *personally* fill it up with the substance of what *I know to be true* about the Gospel, and I bring to the text all kinds of theological formulations in my mind that I've learned over the years to more fully believe its substance. First, I desire to know what the text actually says and means (so I want to be a good interpreter of the text, and properly use hermeneutics to come to conclusions about it. And then I bring to *that meaning* other texts which mean the same thing, or add important information to that text to help me understand it as it sits within the bounds of the truth of God.[11] For example, the Gospel includes information about who God is (who the Son of God is), his Son (who is Christ? And what does it mean that he is God's Son?), the work of God in redemption (the love and justice of God), the giving of Christ fulfilling the law, and "giving" includes the mode of sacrifice in this context of John 3:16, the kind of sacrifice given (that he *gave* himself), there must be a reason *why* Christ gave himself (concerning original sin, the breaking of the covenant, and breaking God's law), and who Christ gave himself for. In other words, there is *much* to the content of the Gospel in order to understand the "simple" Gospel and information contained in the exercise of faith from a

---

[11] We call this the analogy of Scripture, which interprets Scripture by Scripture. The Scriptures in that light cannot contradict one another, and must be in harmony with the whole teaching of the Bible.

regenerate heart (I've assumed much here because I am reading my own theological convictions into the idea of what comprises the Gospel!). But this message of God's Messiah to save his people and deliver them from bondage, this good news, this must turn into a conviction based on testimony which, then, includes *trust*. Interestingly, John 3:16 does *not* talk about repentance. Nor does it define who God is. Nor does it define who this "Son" is. What is belief? How does believing in this way differ from the belief of demons? What is *the world?* Is it the earth? It is the nations of the earth collectively? Is it all men from all time no matter who they are, (Pharaoh and Judas), that God loves? What kind of love is this? Is it electing love? Is it a love "of the creature" as man made in the image of God? There are, in fact, a whole host of questions like this when any verse is used to "sum up" the Gospel because the Gospel is larger than any one verse. That is why God did not give the world one, single verse to cling to, but a very large bible, with many books, and lots of information both about himself, his law, his character, his Son, his Spirit, his church, his work in the world, and all kinds of other truths that Scripture teaches. It is also important to note here that God gave the Old Testament first, before he gave the New Testament in the fullness of time.

Is it a "bad thing" to try and summarize the Gospel? Not at all. But one must necessarily understand that when summaries of the Gospel are given, then the recipient on the receiving end of the Gospel, given in its summary, may be "short changed" to the truths that accompany saving faith. For example, if I were to go to Peru and preach to indigenous people there (which I have done) who know little to nothing of the Gospel, and may have, even, never *heard* the name "Jesus," much less the truths of the Trinity, Scripture, salvation and the like, when I say to them, (or when Jesus says to them in Scripture), "Repent for the Kingdom of heaven is at hand," or, "For God so loves the world..." then the information they have to "fill in" *does not exist.* They are learning these things for the very first time. My "assumed truths" that stand behind those words, actually do not exist *for them yet.* They have never heard of the law of God (though it is written on their heart). They have never heard of the fall of man, (though they are fallen). They have never heard of Jesus Christ, about saving faith, what repentance actually is, *etc.* They do not have the informing knowledge of what those things *mean*, which are, in fact, things Christians take for granted when they ask a question like, "What is the sum and substance of the Gospel?"

As it concerned Martin Luther, it is commented, "Henceforth the doctrine of justification by faith alone was for him to the end of life the sum and substance of the gospel, the heart of theology, the central truth of Christianity, the article of the standing or falling church."[12] Is *this* the substance of the Gospel? Is

---

[12] Miller, Arthur, *Miller's Church History*, (Ages software, 2000), 104.

justification by faith alone the substance of the good news? Thomas Ridgley said, "in the Savior's satisfaction only lies the reason, why his suffering together with his resurrection, are everywhere represented to us as the sum and substance of the gospel."[13] Ridgley does not mention justification. Is the Gospel *not* justification? John Owen said, "the whole work of the mediation of Christ, ... is the sum and substance of the gospel."[14] The *whole work* of the mediation of Christ is the sum and substance of the Gospel? That's quite a lot! What would *that* consist in? It would include just about everything that concerns Christ as Mediator in every facet as Prophet, Priest and King. Ursinus, in his commentary on the *Heidelberg Catechism* says, "The sum and substance of the gospel, or of those things which are to be believed, is the Apostles' Creed, which we here subjoin."[15] This is further interesting, since the sum and substance of the Gospel, according to him, is *the Apostle's Creed*. What is contained in it? *Quite a lot.* There is information in the *creed* about God the Father, Son and Spirit, the Trinity, creation, all the Son's work, his incarnation, life, suffering, death, resurrection and ascension, eternal life, life after death, the church, the communion of saints, the general resurrection, and more. In fact, interestingly, it

---

[13] Ridgley, Thomas. *The Works of Thomas Ridgley,* Volume 2, (Philadelphia, PA: Woodrow, 1814) 295.

[14] Owen, John, *Hebrews,* Volume 3, (Edinburgh: Banner of Truth Trust, 1998) 520.

[15] Ursinus, Zacharias, *The Commentary of the Heidelberg Catechism,* (Cincinnati, OH: P. Bucher Publisher, 1851) 116.

does *not* mention repentance. But Jesus preached a Gospel *of repentance*. Is the *Apostle's Creed* a good summation, then, of the Gospel? Yes, it is, even though it does not cover everything. We can ask directly: Does the *Apostle's Creed* cover all doctrine concerning the Gospel directly? No, it doesn't, and no good preacher or theologian would ever say it does. But that does not mean it is not a good summary of accepted Christian truths surrounding the Gospel. Ulrich Zwingli made the Gospel "simpler" by saying, "the sum and substance of the Gospel [is], namely, that He [Christ] was sent from heaven to suffer death for poor mortals."[16] So, what? No repentance? No belief? No resurrection? Can the Gospel be the Gospel without a resurrection? Thomas Brooks said, "That he [Christ] is freely offered in the gospel. So far as I know my own heart, I do through mercy heartily consent that he only shall be my Savior; not my works or duties, which I do only in obedience to him. If I know my heart, I would be ruled by his word and Spirit. Behold, in a few words, [is] the sum and substance of the gospel."[17] Is the Gospel, then, contained in our *feelings?* Thomas Goodwin, another Westminster Divine, commenting on Ephesians said, "That in the ages to come he might shew the exceeding riches of his grace in his kindness toward us through Christ Jesus," (Eph.

---

[16] Zwingli, Huldreich, *The Latin Works and the Correspondence of Huldreich Zwingli,* Volume 3, (Philadelphia, PA: The American Society of Chruch History, 1929) 128.

[17] Brooks, Thomas, *The Works of Thomas Brooks,* Volume 3, (Carlisle, PA: Banner of Truth Trust, 1980) 261.

2:7), said this was "the sum and substance of the Gospel."[18] John Calvin said, "...this is the substance of the gospel, that God wishes those to repent whom he reconciles by gratuitous pardon. For he is appeased by us only when he makes us new creatures in Christ, and regenerates us by his Spirit; as it is said in Isaiah, God will be propitious to the people who shall have returned from their iniquity." That's a theological mouthful![19] Are all these ideas *the substance* of the Gospel? Calvin further comments on Paul's preaching in Romans where Calvin says, "He calls the gospel the *preaching of Jesus Christ*, inasmuch as the whole sum and substance of it is no doubt included in the knowledge of Christ."[20] The knowledge of Christ is the substance of the Gospel? *How much knowledge is that?*

I must make a notation here so that you, reader, are not confused. Keep in mind, asking, "what is the sum and substance of the Gospel," is *not* the same thing as asking *how much of the Gospel* will *the Holy Spirit use* to regenerate a new soul. Nor is it the same question, how much of the Gospel must be believed *in order to be* justified by faith alone. The question we are dealing with, surrounds *a summary of the Gospel of Jesus*

---

[18] Goodwin, Thomas, *The Works of Thomas Goodwin, D.D.,* Volume 2, Ed. John C. Miller. (Edinburgh: James Nichol, 1861-67; reprinted., Eureka, Calif: Tanski Publications, 1996), 231.

[19] Calvin, John, *Commentary on the First Twenty Chapters of the Book of the Prophet Ezekiel,* Volume 2, (Bellingham, WA: Logos Bible Software, 2010), 180.

[20] Calvin, John, *Commentary on the Epistle of Paul the Apostle to the Romans,* (Bellingham, WA: Logos Bible Software, 2010), 553.

Christ, not, what is the amount of Scriptural data the Holy Spirit needs to regenerate a soul?

I hope, at this point, you are starting to get the point of my questions. The Gospel, in its *sum and substance,* or the way on God's part God was in Christ reconciling the world to himself, contains a great amount of information. Preachers are, "supposed to make this simple." Or *are* they? Understandable, yes, but oversimplistic to the point of losing its sum and substance? *Never.* One preacher who debated with me about this many years ago, said, "whatever the penitent thief on the cross knew is the sum and substance of the Gospel." "Ok, that's fair," I said. *What did he believe?* That's where things got sticky for this preacher. One would assume that the thief just believed that Jesus is Lord, and believing in that *is enough.* But take note, the thief did not mention, nor is it recorded, that he believed God loved him. He did not mention sacrifice, or substitutionary atonement. He did not mention the incarnation. He did not mention that Christ was both God and man, one person in two natures. He did not mention a whole number of important biblical truths contained *in* the Gospel. Here are all his words: first to the other thief on the cross next to him, "Dost not thou fear God, seeing thou art in the same condemnation? And we indeed justly; for we receive the due reward of our deeds: but this man hath done nothing amiss." There is a lot of information in these words. The thief was *taught* well in his synagogue growing up. Once God's

Holy Spirit melted the thief's heart by sovereign, regenerating power, the truth of the Scriptures *he had learned* came flowing out. In this part of his statement he mentions the fear of God, condemnation, justice, and even a reward for works "remembering him" in comparison to Jesus Christ who had "done nothing wrong" (which argues his understanding of covenant theology), the sinless Christ, (which argues his understanding as a Jew of what *mediation* is). Then he turned to Jesus and said, "Lord, remember me when thou comest into thy kingdom." He called him "Lord." He mentioned being "remembered" as it relates to Christ's Lordship, which argues a whole host of theological doctrines. He mentions the coming of Christ into his Kingdom (but no mention of God's love to the world?). His "kingdom theology" argues a vast array of theological doctrines. Then Jesus said back to him, "Verily I say unto thee, today shalt thou be with me in paradise," (Luke 23:40-43). King Jesus speaks to his newly converted servant and tells him he will be in "paradise" with him this very day. In that passage, as much as people would like to think it is a single "simple" truth that the thief believed, he certainly was theologically literate as a Jew, and knew much even though he was a "thief" hanging on a cross. In fact, even Jesus' response catered to the thief's knowledge, in that Jesus said he would be in *paradise* with Christ "this very day." He did not use the term "heaven" but instead recollected the garden paradise (an allusion to the

Covenant of Works in the original garden paradise) of Genesis 2, referencing where Christ *fulfills* the Covenant of Works, as Lord in his atonement. He assumed the thief knew exactly what he meant when he referenced the garden in those particular words.

So, this pastor who debated me years ago was a bit aggravated at my questions to him (both publicly and by way of email), because he saw, in frustration, that his view of, "The Gospel is just one thing," was *not* accurate. What this fellow did, was confused the amount of information the Holy Spirit uses to regenerate the heart in hearing the preached word, with the "sum and substance of the Gospel." As I have asked these initial questions, he saw both those ideas as the same thing, (and the substance of the Gospel, in light of what the Spirit uses to save a man in regeneration, are *not* the same thing). Those two things *are very different.* There is more to the sum and substance of the Gospel than "one thing," or a "simple child-like conversion experience".[21] Even in a minister's explanation of the

---

[21] Even in this fellow's position, he was so upset with me, he wrote a short article claiming I had "perverted the Gospel." This is because he was (is?) confused about the doctrines of God's free grace in Jesus Christ, in comparison to (his words) "trusting in Jesus Christ for salvation," in comparison to the "simple child-like faith" he was trying to espouse. In fact, his problem was that he was espousing a retreat from Gospel-content, and trying to allow salvation to occur by divorcing truth from being saved. This is *impossible.* He confused the amount of truth the holy Spirit would use to save a person, from a summary or explanation of the Gospel itself. The question was posed, "Can a person who never hears or understands the doctrines of grace go to heaven?" But, this would be the same as asking, "Can a person who never hears the Gospel go to heaven?"

Gospel, such a minister can't say everything to be said every time he preaches; and many misunderstand what I means to "preach Christ crucified" because of their lack of theological precision.[22] Gospel proclamation builds based on conceived notions that are layered upon layers of theological teaching *over time*. Again, argue from the Old Testament to the New Testament in this. It's the way God has always explained himself and his word. He took a long time to get to the Gospel of Matthew from Genesis 3:15. It was a span of thousands of years. This does not detract on the work of the Spirit of God to regenerate a person in the Old Testament, or for that matter, in the New Testament. But it does set down that Gospel content *has* content, and a certain amount of that Gospel content must be believed in order to believe the Gospel (towards *conversion*). Again, this is a

---

This is what this fellow *missed completely*...and just think, our pulpits are filled with such people today all across the world. They have a zeal for God, but not according to knowledge (Romans 10:2).
[22] They will "claim" strive only to preach *Christ and him crucified*, but they forget *what* Christ preached, *what* John the Baptist preached, *what* the disciples preached and how the message of the Kingdom explains all this. They do not understand Paul's arguments leading up to his proclamation that he will "preach Christ crucified" which he longed to do, and set out to do. This is because their Gospel seems to start with Romans and Galatians, instead of Genesis, and they *work backwards* filling in their own notions to what the Gospel actually is. This is why dispensational preachers who work backwards in the bible are often a *hindrance* to the Gospel and not a help. Whatever Abraham believed about the Gospel, he was born again. Whatever Samson believed about the Gospel, he was born again. Whatever David believed about the Gospel, he was born again. For, "unless a man is born again he cannot enter the Kingdom of heaven," as our Savior instructed.

different question than how many Scriptures the Spirit uses to *regenerate* a heart (towards *regeneration*). What it does is place that regenerate heart in the midst of *believing*, and what is believed must be the Gospel, and the Gospel is more than one thing. One will prove out the other.

It is not my intention here to argue with people who say, "But what about the Gospel given in Genesis 3:15?" "Is that Gospel enough?" or any derivation of that argument at any time in church history in some *cliff-noted* form. It is true, this is the Gospel, "And I will put enmity between thee and the woman, and between thy seed and her seed; it shall bruise thy head, and thou shalt bruise his heel," (Gen. 3:15). But this proto-Gospel, this *first announcement* of the Gospel, is housed in shadows.[23] Christians understand that it refers to Christ, and his power in sacrifice, and the salvation of his people in the seed of the woman (covenant salvation). But the reason they know it, is because they assume certain truths annexed to Genesis 3:15 by way of filling that verse up by, 1) good hermeneutics and interpretation, and, 2) the analogy of faith which theologically fills in all their perceived understandings of what that verse means in light of scripture. They fill that verse up substantially with their own

---

[23] "...in and by those promises, types, and sacrifices, wherein he was revealed, and signified to be the seed of the woman which should bruise the serpent's head, and the Lamb slain from the beginning of the world, being yesterday and today the same, and forever." *The 1647 Westminster Confession of Faith*, 8:6.

understanding of what the Gospel is. I would even argue against them a bit in this. They are, in fact, not as keen and aware as Eve was when she said, not but a few verses later, "I have gotten [the man] from the LORD," (Gen. 4:1). She thought the Messiah had come when Cain, her firstborn, was born. She thought that original Gospel message was fulfilled *right there*. Why would God wait around to answer such a subline promise of good news? She thought Cain was "the man" from the Lord which he spoke about to fix this awful fall that has occurred. Still, biblical knowledge gives verses in the Bible content. Understanding what is being said, or preached, or stated, is very important (and in this way, hermeneutics is very important.)

So, what do we do here in this introduction? Do we *give up* on giving the sum and substance of the Gospel because the Gospel is more than one thing? Do we just turn to the *Sum of Saving Knowledge*,[24] and go with that? What I intend here is to think about the basic *principles* of the Gospel as Christ would have thought about them from the Old Testament. He did not have creeds and confessions to draw from. He certainly was familiar with rabbinical texts that commented on the

---

[24] *The Sum of Saving Knowledge* was written in light of the Westminster Confession by David Dickson. It covers, the woeful condition which all men are in by nature, through breaking of the covenant of works. The remedy provided for the elect in Jesus Christ by the covenant of grace. The means appointed to make them partakers of this covenant. The blessings which are effectually conveyed to the elect by these means." Again, this too is an excellent summary.

Old Testament by some of his statements and parables which he incorporated *even with certain changes* in his preaching of the word, but his Gospel presentation and the declaring of the Father (John 1:18) came solely from the Scriptures in the Old Testament. So, my intention is to *summarize* the Gospel into five main principles, drawn from the Old Testament "Gospel" of Isaiah. Certainly, I could have used a whole host of various passages, but Isaiah holds in it some of the most poignant Gospel depictions that any of the prophets set forth. In fact, there are some passages that you, the reader, would think I *should* use in Isaiah, and I don't. All of this was purposefully set down in this work, to deal with certain unavoidable concepts and conclusions that all tie into the sum and substance of the Gospel.[25] With all that said, let's look to the first principle.

---

[25] I need to give a disclaimer at this point. Some may think that I ought to deal with "The Kingdom of God" since that is what John, Jesus, and his disciples actually *preached*, (where his disciples were particularly *commanded to preach* "that message" when Christ sent them out). I have saved that topic for another work (my book *The Kingdom of Heaven is Upon You*), which will in fact, cover that idea fully. This work, and that work, will be complementary, when combined together. But the absence of that full-orbed idea, will not hinder this present study.

Principle 1:
Behold Your God

"Comfort ye, comfort ye my people, saith your God. Speak ye comfortably to Jerusalem, and cry unto her, that her warfare is accomplished, that her iniquity is pardoned: for she hath received of the LORD'S hand double for all her sins. The voice of him that crieth in the wilderness, Prepare ye the way of the LORD, make straight in the desert a highway for our God. Every valley shall be exalted, and every mountain and hill shall be made low: and the crooked shall be made straight, and the rough places plain: And the glory of the LORD shall be revealed, and all flesh shall see it together: for the mouth of the LORD hath spoken it. The voice said, Cry. And he said, What shall I cry? All flesh is grass, and all the goodliness thereof is as the flower of the field: The grass withereth, the flower fadeth: because the spirit of the LORD bloweth upon it: surely the people is grass. The grass withereth, the flower fadeth: but the word of our God shall stand for ever. O Zion, that bringest good tidings, get thee up into the high mountain; O Jerusalem, that bringest good tidings, lift up thy voice with strength; lift it up, be not afraid; say unto the cities of Judah, Behold your God! Behold, the Lord GOD will come with strong hand, and his arm shall rule for him: behold, his reward is with him, and his work before him," (Isaiah 40:1-10).

Many find this section of Isaiah as a turning point. It has been said by many good preachers, that the first 39 chapters of Isaiah correspond to the Old Testament and that the last 29 chapters correspond to the New Testament. This may be *somewhat* of a stretch, because Isaiah deals with a lot of Gospel truths in this pre-Gospel of the Kingdom of God, and "the coming of the Messiah" is mixed in his writings in the various chapters up to this point; it's not so cut and dry to divide his book in that light. However, there is something to be said of this great turning point here in chapter 40. It seems that it does mark *a kind* of turning point in both the mood and message of the prophet overall. Here is found the pending coming of the enthroned King to the church. Currently, Israel was in Mesopotamian exile, and the prophet turns to encourage the church to both be comforted by the announcement, and encourage them to announce God's coming. The good news here is set in the announcement that God does not leave the church alone. The Messiah is coming, a new day for Jerusalem, having been forgiven in the Anointed One of the burden of all guilt stemming from the fall.

With the coming of forgiveness, God is seen as coming to the city and to the temple in all his glory. The world will know that God is in his temple and in his city, in the coming of the Messiah and his church, in the coming of forgiveness, in the coming of the establishments of his reign and power over the fall.

Isaiah will in fact say later, such good news is set on the reality that, "Thy God reigneth," (Isaiah 52:7).

Such a coming of the Kingdom of God, the very foundations of the news and the hearts that should run after it, do not set themselves in the midst of anything that men can do; for all is pointing to the great King. Isaiah is not instructing the people to work out something on their own, or trust in their own frail human capacities which fade like a flower, or like grass, but they depend solely on the word of God, the promises of God, the Logos of God.[1] God has given his word and promises, and he will bring forgiveness, and he will sustain them. He has instructed them in the first few verses to be *comforted.* This is the proclamation of John the Baptist in the wilderness heralding the coming of King Jesus, the Lamb who takes away the sin of the world.[2] Isaiah's entire passage is set on not only the release from Babylonian captivity, but release from sin through the Messiah. They are comforted by the coming of God in their midst, which speaks of the triumph of God over the fall in his rule and reign as the sovereign King.

Specifically, as the triumphal entry into Jerusalem by the Anointed Messiah,[3] so we find its prophecy here. There, valleys are exalted, and hills are brought low, speaking prophetically of the smooth

---

[1] "All flesh is grass," (Isa. 40:6). "The grass withereth, the flower fadeth," (Isa. 40:8).
[2] John 1:29.
[3] Matthew 21:5.

streets of the way of the Messiah as the streets are adorned with the praises of the people, and the palm branches which fill in the holes and level the mountains as Jesus comes riding as King into the holy city.[4] The pot holes of the streets will be made flat, the bumps in the road will be made flat, and the Messiah will ride in on the palm branches of the people on the colt of a donkey in triumph, and "blessed is he who comes in the name of the Lord;" for he is God's Messiah and King, he comes in riding on the praises of the people; and what is Isaiah's message about this?

Isaiah says, "Behold your God." "The grass withereth, the flower fadeth: but the word of our God shall stand for ever." Yes, it is true, like God, the word of God stands forever. The ungodly think that what they do matters; in other words, that all their hard work pertains to some kind of good thing or good work they do as they live life, which will endure for some kind of legacy. They believe that their words are lasting, what they do in life will preserve them, what their works are will be forever. But, they are like the grass, like the picked flower. It dies quickly. The word of God remains, but all the works of men are fading like grass that withers. Therefore, remember and believe that the strength of this word conquers all things, for it alone remains. Flowers, grass, flesh of all kinds, and people will fall and sink into nothing; decay, disaster, in a word, die and come to nothing in death. Visible death is seen

---

[4] John 12:13.

in its withering of life. If one desires to remain, by implication, this one looks to the word, and in the word they will not be dried up, for it stands. They are to cling to the Word of God that will stand forever and cause them to rejoice, and what is this rejoicing?

Verse 9 says, "O Zion, that bringest good tidings, get thee up into the high mountain; O Jerusalem, that bringest good tidings, lift up thy voice with strength; lift it up, be not afraid; say unto the cities of Judah, Behold your God!" "O Zion," is the church. In this, God makes known his mind through the prophet for the comfort of his people. The church is called a garden, a sealed fountain, as Song 4:12; a vineyard, Matt. 20:1; a house, 1 Tim. 3:15; a city, Psa. 46:4; Isa. 60:14; a mountain, Psa. 2:6. Mountains are high, and strong. They metaphorically are nearer to heaven than other things. What do these high mountains do? They raise the voice up, "that bringest good tidings." These good tidings are heralded by preachers in the church, but interestingly Zion is instructed as a church to herald the good news by way of both their visibility and standing, and in their work of living out the good tidings as much as preachers are to proclaim it. This word, "bear good news," or, "bear good tidings," is translated into *euangellion*, or what the New Testament refers to as *evangelism*. Sometimes, the word "Jerusalem" is taken for those elders who were to teach and encourage the people to discern the truth and follow the way of God, gathering in all the people, even those outside the city walls. Here the prophet presses and encouragement of this visible manifestation of the good news, and the heralding of this good news in the life of the church; the way they live and what they know to be true. "...get thee up into the high mountain; O Jerusalem, that bringest good tidings, lift up thy voice with strength; lift it up, be not afraid." All flesh is grass and the Word alone stands, and yet, now follows an exhortation where they are to hold steadfastly the word of God, which they have come to know and not fall into ruin.

The church is to be a herald of good tidings, for the church is commanded to do so. The church should teach one another and then publish the glory and praise of God to the world through heralds. O Zion, O thou (whosoever you are, Prophet or Apostle) that *bringest good tidings to Zion*, it is not merely the herald, but first the receiver of these good tidings, as she is in Isa. 52:7. Zion is the speaker or publisher, and the cities of Judah the hearers. They are *heralds* of good tidings, good things, following the Hebrew מְבַשֶּׂרֶת. The stress lies on the words *that bringest good tidings.* This Hebrew idea (בָּשַׂר) means to proclaim joyful and happy reports. Since the church has been well informed and well taught, she must proclaim and urge joyful tidings to one another, and others who do not have this report. They are even instructed to go up onto a high mountain to proclaim this word. They are to be visible as a city set on a hill. The world desires to stifle the church, but the church must publish good tidings, on the tops of mountains, to set down the dominion of God in its power. Arise above the world, teach them the truth, demonstrate the good news, and make disciples of all the nations.

What are they to do? "...lift up your voice with strength," meaning *with great force*. "Do not be afraid, because you have the eternal Word which is sure and steadfast." It stands, and it stands because God stands, he is unchanging and eternal,[5] as his word is, so do not fear. In fact, "Be not afraid." Preachers often do not exercise being the voice of God in the manner they are required because they are afraid of men. They fear what men will think of them, and in our culture today, they will be deposed by the people.[6] Is there cause for such fear? The church as a whole is exhorted to be *not afraid.* And what is the content of the message that they are to herald or bring concerning the good tidings of God's eternal word of the triumphant King coming into their midst? It is in this passage, a general proclamation, the first and primary proclamation, that is said, "Say to the cities of Judah: Behold your God!" This is the *substance* of their message.

"Behold your God!" The word "behold" has the force, "to look to." It stresses the following word, "God". It points the finger to God, it displays him, it attracts attention to him. Promote God, promote him. God is the

---

[5] "For I am the LORD, I change not; therefore ye sons of Jacob are not consumed," (Mal. 3:6).
[6] I have personally seen this time and time again.

God of all. Behold your God. Promote and behold God alone. Preach God alone. Preach mercy and grace in the Messiah alone. Preach the coming of God's kingdom alone. Preach peace alone through God's power and dominion over the fall. Preach comfort to the city in the midst of the fall. *Behold Your God.* Ungodly men preach the doctrines and works of men, their own works and their own righteousness. The herald in God's church must avoid that kind of teaching and preach the Anointed Savior alone; and the church must visibly demonstrate that God alone is to be praised.[7] In God alone rests all salvation, and this salvation is to know that God is there, *to behold him.* Say this to the cities of Judah, because the Word shall go forth from Zion and Jerusalem, it will be manifest, not hidden, speak to all and teach them because they need the eternal word for eternal life, and this is that which speaks of the reigning King.

Verse 10 says, "Behold, the Lord GOD will come with strong hand, and his arm shall rule for him: behold, his reward is with him, and his work before him." Behold this almighty God. He comes with might,[8] with a strong hand, a hand of dominion and absolute authority and power. He comes with might, and those who are weak

---

[7] "For I determined not to know any thing among you, save Jesus Christ, and him crucified," (1 Cor. 2:2). Is this one thing? Or, is Paul winding up at the end of his Gospel-argument about what the Gospel actually teaches? Is this only one part of the Gospel? Consider this in light of the *introductory chapter.*

[8] "The mighty God," (Isa. 9:6).

may trust in the power of God for salvation to overthrow the works of the fall on their heart, mind and soul. Those who are fainthearted, those who are weak, can rely on the mighty power of God.[9] It not only transforms them, but it aids them in being lights on a hill as a church. It aids even the preacher and heralds of the church in proclamation. It is not done in mere words of wisdom, but in the power of the Spirit and his might; not by might, nor by power, *but by my Spirit.* God even comes with a reward to his faithful. Though the church is beckoned to great heights of proclamation, and though they may feel like they are despised in the world, behold, the Lord's might will be with them. He is the one that makes his word not return to him void. It will accomplish all his pleasure, and it will do its work in their midst.

The power of God is seen in the proclamation of the word by weak vessels, knowing full well that when they are weak, so, he is strong. It is, in fact, God's word, God's power, *not* theirs. It is in fact a point that preachers ought to be strict on that it is God's word, not their cleverness or ability, that saves the day. The Lord comes with mighty power in weak vessels. It is a mighty word with a very strong arm. The power of the strong arm is metaphorical, that the strength of God will not abandon those that endure under his word, with his word, for his glory, to point out to the world, behold your God. His power will be with them. And even this,

---

[9] "...let the weak say, I am strong," (Joel 3:10).

"Behold, his reward is with him." This reward, or his *work's earned wages*, is something God must provide. All the outcome of the work comes with him. *Reward* here means all of the fruit of the good news, which shall not be preached in vain and will not return empty because it is God's word and it accomplishes God's purpose.[10] Its reward comes from the Anointed one who comes in with a strong arm. It is as if God is saying, as Luther said, "It is impossible that the Word should not necessarily prosper where it is preached. Your labor will not be in vain, because His reward will be there, that is, it will succeed. For recompense denotes the fruit itself, as the recompense of the field is the crop, and the recompense of the vine is grapes. In this way he consoles us so that we do not despair of the success of the Word, because the reward and recompense, the power and strength of the Lord, will bring it about. This is what His reward and recompense means, the fruit and promotion of the Gospel."[11]

And what shall he do? Verse 11, "He shall feed his flock like a shepherd: he shall gather the lambs with his arm, and carry them in his bosom, and shall gently lead those that are with young." Without going too far into some of the benefits, for this is a very pregnant verse,

---

[10] "So shall my word be that goeth forth out of my mouth: it shall not return unto me void, but it shall accomplish that which I please, and it shall prosper in the thing whereto I sent it," (Isa. 55:11).

[11] Luther, Martin, *Luther's Works*, Volume 17, <u>Lectures on Isaiah: Chapters 40-66.</u> J.J. Pelikan, H. C. Oswald, & H. T. Lehmann, Eds. (Saint Louis, MO: Concordia Publishing House, 1999) 12–16.

make note that God through the Messiah will feed his flock like a Shepherd.[12] God will bring success through the word, through the Messiah, as a Shepherd, so that it will encourage both the strong and the weak. He will feed his sheep, believers and those instructed by beholding God. And he will gather the lambs. He grazes the hearty sheep in the fields, but carries the young lambs in his arms, for in the church there are the strong and the weak in faith, and a good herald of the word looks after them both. He gently leads those that are with young, that is, he deals with them as they can bear it.

The first principle of the good tidings of the Gospel is to behold the mighty God, *that God exists*.

The Gospel was of an everlasting determination by God who reveals himself in both creation and providence, but more clearly in his good tidings. The only way men can know that God exists is if he *reveals* himself. He is seen in creation, but that is not enough; he must draw men to himself in a very particular way. *The 1647 Westminster Confession* states the following in 1:1, "Although the light of nature, and the works of creation and providence, do so far manifest the goodness, wisdom, and power of God, as to leave men inexcusable (Psalm 19:1-3; Romans 1:19-20; 1:32 with 2:1; 2:14-15); yet they are not sufficient to give that knowledge of God,

---

[12] Shepherd imagery is extremely prominent and important as it pertain to both God and Christ throughout Scripture. This is especially true in the psalms, Jeremiah, Zechariah, Ezekiel and in the Gospel of John.

and of his will, which is necessary unto salvation (1 Corinthians 1:21; 2:13-14)." God's works of creation and providence[13] manifest that God exists, but they do not give precepts, commands or directions on how man is to live before God either practically, or after the fall, savingly. In the works of creation and providence God manifests himself clearly. "Because that which may be known of God is manifest in them; for God hath shewed it unto them. For the invisible things of him from the creation of the world are clearly seen, being understood by the things that are made, even his eternal power and Godhead; so that they are without excuse," (Rom. 1:19-20). God's invisible nature and eternal power have been clearly perceived from the creation of the world. But what of his love, and grace and mercy? What of his saving power decreed in light of the fall? What of the Trinity, or the coming of God's fellow, the Messiah to redeem? Creation and providence in natural revelation cannot suffice to demonstrate God's eternal love in Christ for his elect, nor the manner of God's will in salvation after the fall. Creation and providence do not have the accompanying power of the Spirit of God which regenerates fallen man to see the sweetness of Christ, and neither general creation nor common natural providence contain anything concerning the mysteries of salvation, and God's mercy through the death and

---

[13] *The 1647 Westminster Shorter Catechism* in question 8 asks, "How doth God execute his decrees?" The Answer, "God executeth his decrees in the works of creation and providence," (Psa. 148:8; Isa. 40:26; Dan. 4:35; Acts 4:24-28; Rev. 4:11).

resurrection of Christ. Yet, nature itself teaches that God exists and that he is to be glorified. "The heavens declare the glory of God; and the firmament showeth his handywork," (Psa. 19:1). The Creator is to be glorified by creation alone, but there is more. In turn, he will be a rewarder of those who seek him (Heb. 11:6). Those who seek him will worship him. Nature teaches that the soul is immortal, it desires to have the vacuum of its existence filled with something that satisfies it. *The theology of Jesus Christ* is what fills that void, by the power of the Spirit, through reception of God's word. In this *beholding God* is what fills that void, to see him and to trust that his way of abundant life is best. Nature teaches that the rational creature can only be satisfied in God alone, to whom all theology points. Certainly, nature shows that God exists, and of what nature God is, invisible attributes and divine power, but nature does not tell men who he is with regard to the persons of the Godhead and their economy or the way they exist, how the Godhead governs the universe and how God save sinners. It does not contain all of God's character, nor does it reveal the mystery of the gospel. Good tidings of beholding God are completely concealed in nature. Francis Turretin said, "Nature merely displays the works of creation and providence (Ps. 19:13; Acts 14:15-17; 17:23-28; Rom. 1:19-20), but does not rise up to the works of redemption and grace which can become known to us by the word alone (Rom. 10:17; 16:25-26)."[14] That God exists, that he is to be beheld, is to be proclaimed, and that mightily in this, that one is to behold him. "In the beginning *God* created the heaven and the earth," (Gen. 1:1). This verse, to most historic preachers and theologians, is the most important verse in the bible. It presumes on the existence of God from the outset, and sets the entirety of the biblical record on the reality *that* God exists. *That God exists*, and, *that he has revealed himself in his holy word,* is the foundation of the first principle. Men come to behold him through his revealed word. It must be proclaimed by heralds because men are fallen, and the truth of the natural creation is warped and twisted by man's original sin, so it needs to be communicated. He is unable to come to any saving knowledge by creation or natural providence; he cannot find a Savior there when it rains or when the sun shines, but gropes in the dark. He is merely rendered without excuse to God's existence and the requirement to worship this God seen in the works of creation.

That God exists is to be proclaimed from the Scriptures. Since the mind has been darkened, man is inclined to doubt this God. Even Christians doubt from time to time what God is providentially doing in their life, what his *plan* is for them.[15] That what he does is all

---

[14] Turretin, Francis, *Institutes of Elenctic Theology*, Volume 1, (Phillipsburg, NJ: Presbyterian and Reformed Publishing Company, 1992-94) 56.

[15] "O my God, I cry in the daytime, but thou hearest not," (Psa. 22:2).

good and just even in difficult times.[16] God's word in the Holy Scriptures is called *the Word of God.* In Romans 3:2 it is stated, "Unto them were committed the oracles of God." God condescended to man and has revealed the way of truth by the revelation of the Spirit to move and carry men to write down what he requires of man, and what his duty is before him as Creator and Governor of the world. "God, who at sundry times and in divers manners spake in time past unto the fathers by the prophets, hath in these last days spoken unto us by His Son," (Heb. 1:1–2). Such a revelation of God to men was *necessary.* The written word is a light which illuminates the path men must take to find God and live in godliness. "Thy word is a lamp unto my feet, and a light unto my path," (Psa. 119:105). When people hide both the path to God and the life of God in the soul of man, if they speak not according to the law and to the testimony, "it is because there is no light in them," (Isa. 8:20). In this way, the existence of the written word is a necessity. According to the text at hand, the written word declares the necessity of men to *behold your God,* and that beholding your God directs men to the Messiah that God has sent to save them from death and hell; and the very first thing that God declares in his word is that he exists, "In the beginning, God," in order to behold him.

---

[16] "And we know that all things work together for good to them that love God, to them who are the called according to his purpose," (Rom. 8:28).

Further, it concerns the Kingdom of God as revealed by the Messiah, to come in the flesh, Behold your God![17] By way of prophetic utterance, the Messiah *is* God, for these good tidings center on God first, and second, on his coming to save sinful men out of the bondage they have fallen into. *The Gospel does not center on sinners, but God.*[18] Sinners reap benefits from the existence of this God. Sinners reap benefits from the coming of the Christ. Beholding God points to the Christ in which is, "all good things" and the only way to behold the Father, and this is by him who is, "altogether lovely," (Song of Songs 5:16). What was the effect of the apostle's ministry, who, after Christ's ascension, were sent forth to preach *about him?* Is preaching about Christ the same as preaching about the Kingdom of God? And how do these two ideas mix together? It

---

[17] *The 1647 Westminster Confession of Faith*, 8:2, says, "The Son of God, the second person in the Trinity, being very and eternal God, of one substance, and equal with the Father, did, when the fulness of time was come, take upon him man's nature, with all the essential properties and common infirmities thereof, yet without sin: being conceived by the power of the Holy Ghost in the womb of the Virgin Mary, of her substance. So that two whole, perfect, and distinct natures, the Godhead and the manhood, were inseparably joined together in one person, without conversion, composition, or confusion. Which person is very God and very man, yet one Christ, the only mediator between God and man."

[18] 1 Samuel. 12:22, "For the LORD will not forsake his people for his great name's sake: because it hath pleased the LORD to make you his people." Psalm 23:3, "He restoreth my soul: he leadeth me in the paths of righteousness for his name's sake." Psalm. 143:11, "Quicken me, O LORD, for thy name's sake: for thy righteousness' sake bring my soul out of trouble." Jeremiah. 14:21, "Do not abhor us, for thy name's sake, do not disgrace the throne of thy glory: remember, break not thy covenant with us."

follows in the same prophecy that Isaiah is stating, "O Zion, that bringest good tidings, get thee up into the high mountain; Jerusalem, that bringest good tidings, lift up thy voice with strength: lift it up, be not afraid : say unto the cities of Judah, Behold your God." This message was, "Behold your God!" in its inception. That is, behold the Messiah (Genesis 3), the one who crushes the head of the serpent; behold the Christ, who is your God, the Son of God in his person, the ruler, the rewarder, in whom is eternal life, and the Shepherd of his people,[19] who gives abundant life and makes men happy; these are good tidings to proclaim. This is the God who comes with a strong saving arm to reverse the heinous effects of the fall. This is the One who brings his reward with him to those who will behold him. This is the one who shall feed his flock *like a shepherd.* This is the one who shall gather the lambs with his arm, and carry them in his bosom, and shall gently lead those that are with young regardless of the weakness of their believing state. That God exists, then, presupposes that there is a manner in which he reveals his existence. No one can come to this God, this God of light which no man can access, but by God's means. What was the voice of one crying in the wilderness but, "Behold the Lamb of God!" *behold* the Son of God; *behold* that God exists, and here he is in the personage of the Christ, God wills that men *behold* him who takes away their sin. What

---

[19] "The LORD is my shepherd," (Psa. 23:1). "I am the good shepherd: the good shepherd giveth his life for the sheep," (John 10:11).

was the voice of the apostles in their proclamation of the Christ? "Behold your God!" we preach a Savior to you, who is God. 2 Cor. 4:5-6 says, "For we preach not ourselves, but Christ Jesus the Lord; and ourselves your servants for Jesus' sake. For God who commanded the light to shine out of darkness, hath shined in our hearts, to give the light of the knowledge of the glory of God, in the face of Jesus Christ." That is, behold your God, this is found in the person of the Anointed Savior, and as Zech. 13:7 says, he is God's only *fellow*.[20] He is the image of God, the exact representation of the Father, heralded by Isaiah in this 40th chapter. Behold your God, he will save us, behold your God, he will come and deliver by his strong arm, behold your God, he is the Anointed Savior, behold your God, he is this Jesus, that saves his people from their sins. This is the Lord, and he alone saves, behold him in all his glory. This is where the faith of believers sits, in beholding this God, in beholding this Christ, in this one to believe on.

What is it to behold the Savior, to behold God? What is it to "look to me" and see (using another phrase from Isaiah)[21] that God exists, or that he is to be beheld? It sets supernatural faith on what is proclaimed in the Scripture. No believer ever places faith in something

---

[20] "Awake, O sword, against my shepherd, and against the man that is my fellow, saith the LORD of hosts: smite the shepherd, and the sheep shall be scattered: and I will turn mine hand upon the little ones," (Zech. 13:7).
[21] "Look unto me, and be ye saved, all the ends of the earth: for I am God, and there is none else," (Isa. 45:22).

that they do not know. Faith is not blind, but set on the one that the onlooker beholds by the word. 1 Tim. 3:16 says, "And without controversy, great is the mystery of godliness: God was manifest in the flesh," (or made flesh, or beheld); "justified in the Spirit," or that his Godhead was manifested in the power and act of the resurrection, "preached to the Gentiles, and believed on in the world." Beholding Christ is the way of beholding God. Christ, the God-man, the Son of God in the flesh, is the "prime grand object of all the believers' faith that were in that age of the world; and he is the great mystery and foundation of all Christian religion; and therefore under that notion and apprehension of him, made lively and real to our souls, [and] it is that we must come to him."[22]

The church is to proclaim him to all the world in his infinite goodness and divine comfort in beholding God and his existence. This is the only place divine comfort is found in the midst of the fall. Beholding God, seeing God, is of divine comfort. In preaching, this is found only in the church, taking all advantage of the *highest mountains* to publish it, *per se*, that it may be most and best heard. The general proclamation and the specific message, Isaiah 40, *Behold Your God*, and ... what of him? That he is the King of the Kingdom of God, that, Isaiah 52, "Thy God Reigns," over the fall and can fix the depravity of those that see their spiritual need by

---

[22]Goodwin, Thomas. *The Works of Thomas Goodwin*, Volume 8, Ed. John C. Miller. (Edinburgh: James Nichol, 1861-67; reprinted., Eureka, Calif: Tanski Publications, 1996), 186.

being born of the Spirit. This is true comfort, found in the preaching of the word, seeing Christ clearly; then Christians can live this out in their life by faith. "But without faith it is impossible to please him: for he that cometh to God must believe that he is, and that he is a rewarder of them that diligently seek him," (Heb. 11:6). In Heb 11:6 the concern is with faith "that [God] exists" (ὅτι ἔστιν) and can be found. Romans 9:5ff, ὁ ὢν ἐπὶ πάντων θεός, "God who has power over everything," God whose dominion is *over all.* Faith in God is impossible without a belief in *something.* There is a beholding God in the way God has revealed him and a resting on God by faith as he is revealed.

This first principle, then, that God exists, is quite necessary, and very obvious to the message of good tidings to men, of salvation. Can a person come to behold God if he believes that God doesn't exist? Can a person come to behold God if he believes things contrary to God's revelation of himself? Nor is a person allowed to behold their own fabrication of God. They must believe what God has revealed about himself. If a person believes that God exists as some impersonal force, or merely their own god that is greater than themselves, he will not come to God, nor is he really beholding God; he is not seeing the Messiah. And even by way of the writer of Hebrews, he must believe that God comes as a rewarder of those who diligently seek him. For, to behold him rightly is rewarded by God. This implies that

God is personal; so, to make this personal to you ... consider the following.

There are three kinds of belief systems you must reject. The first is the atheist,[23] who does not want to believe in God and suppresses the truth. At this particular point, some might think that rendering a solid athiestical argument and the Christian response might be warranted or helpful. That *God exists*, and *how* it is so. But that would not, for our purposes, really set down the first principle of God existing in demonstrating the basic fundamental principles of these good tidings, and the reality that God is beheld in a certain light and way. The Bible does not engage on this point, in this Isaiah passage in some kind of atheistical refutation. As if Isaiah said, "behold your God and this is how you can know that God exists, by beholding him without reservation." As the passage demonstrates, the church heralds the message first to Judah, *to the church*. It gives a corrected understanding of the hope and promise of God in his word, and how that hope and promise come forth and is actualized in the Messiah. He is the one that comes to save and comfort you. And so here, in this first principle of the good news, the point to be made is that God is beheld in Christ by real faith in his revealed word and proclamation which you are to believe. God has proclaimed salvation, the day of salvation, and men in

---

[23] "The fool hath said in his heart, There is no God. They are corrupt, they have done abominable works, there is none that doeth good," (Psalm 14:1).

the church, and connected to the church, are to heed God's proclamation with a true faith; the message comes from somewhere. It comes from God, and it is found in his word; it is to be published on high mountains. Though Isaiah has many good things to say to the atheist, as does the whole of Scripture, Isaiah was not written to the atheist, but to the church. Why? "...because the carnal mind is enmity against God: for it is not subject to the law of God, neither indeed can be," (Rom. 8:7).

The course we take on this application is not apologetically, but polemically. It is not to the atheist but to the church; it is to the one sitting there in the pew, not to the one who merely desires to argue about God's existence, or suppress the truth. It is to you, reader, who takes an interest in this God, who desires you to behold him. To not believe in God or what God says about himself is to go directly against our text. God is to be beheld, not suppressed in sinful conceptions of what you hope he is like. Atheists hate God so much that they suppress him in their thoughts (or at least try to). Christians can do this when they reject sound doctrine and substitute what is true in the word with what is false (or what they like); when they go their own way and do not behold God as God has prescribed.[24] To believe something contrary to the truth is to suppress

---

[24] "But the house of Israel will not hearken unto thee; for they will not hearken unto me: for all the house of Israel are impudent and hardhearted," (Ezek. 3:7).

the truth. It is to act atheistically, and this must be rejected.

The hypocrite must be considered for a moment, who is the great pretender of religion.[25] The hypocrite pretends to get into the Kingdom of heaven by thinking that merely believing in God is enough, which prompts him to do or accomplish certain duties that give him an appearance of doing what is right, yet without sincerity. He may be fair in the eyes of others in the church, or even to himself, but in his heart, he is the legalist, the one who works for his salvation. And he does those things he deems are most important, and often, to be seen by himself, or others, but never to please God in obedience. It may certainly be that the hypocrite is sincere in what he does, and even thinks what he does is good and right. But these are the *Judases* of the church. Their hypocrisy is a lie, and they are false professors, who may in fact do very much in the kingdom, and many times even more than what real Christians might do; the Pharisees were very diligent in their works; but they did not have a Savior.

You must not be a hypocrite in your beliefs. To profess something, but not to live a life answerable to that profession, to believe something else, is hypocrisy. Much unbelief still resides in this kind of a fellow who

---

[25] "Ye hypocrites, well did Esaias prophesy of you, saying, This people draweth nigh unto me with their mouth, and honoureth me with their lips; but their heart is far from me. But in vain they do worship me, teaching for doctrines the commandments of men," (Matt. 15:7-9).

is a hypocrite. They have a form of religion, but they deny its power.[26]

You must also reject the devil's kind of belief. Your belief in God must be more than the demons or devils. What do I mean by this? You behold God, according to the truth. You believe that truth; what does the devil believe about God? "Thou believest that there is one God; thou doest well: the devils also believe, and tremble," (James 2:19). James goes on with his reply and takes up the point of having a creed apart from works, belief that God exists (there is one God), a fundamental doctrine (is it not?), but that is not belief and trust in God, it is not which leads God to speak comfort, and eternal life, to you through a Savior. It certainly may be that one has a creed that falls into the realm of truth; many wayward professors say all kinds of true things about God. They may believe many orthodox things about him; and they may be able to recite their catechism. James says, you behold this God, behold he is your God, and you believe this, and in this, *you do well.* That is good, as far as it goes, he is saying, but that is not very far. The demons also believe, *they go that far.* The very same verb πιστευω (*pisteuow*), that people have in believing in God, well, the demons never doubt the fact of God's existence and who he is according to truth. Not only do they believe, but this belief prompts a certain sensible response by them. They shudder (και

---

[26] "Having a form of godliness, but denying the power thereof: from such turn away," (2 Tim. 3:5).

φρισσουσιν [kai phrissousin]). Present active indicative of φρισσω [phrissow], an old onomatopoetic verb meaning to *bristle up, to shudder,* which is only used here in New Testament. It is akin to the Latin *horreo* (*horror,* literally meaning the *standing of the hair on end with terror*). The demons do more than believe in facts. They shudder at it, that belief has a sensible response (a response of *sense*) to them. Devils tremble, but "do you quake," (Isaiah 33:14)? Satan in a certain manner beholds God, (James 2:19), and that Christ is the Son of God, "since you are the Son of God," "I know who you are the holy one of God," the demons said, (Luke 4:34). The devil was there in the beginning as a holy angel hearing with his own ears the seraphim's chant in heaven, "holy, holy, holy," (Isaiah 6:1-4) while the Christ sat enthroned in the highest. The devil is no atheist; he knows the Christ. But nowhere in the bible do you ever find demons accusing themselves of sin, wickedness, examining themselves, and their lack of holiness. Instead, they tempt to it; they challenge the law of God in it, and act in opposition to it, they reject what it requires of them to trust God. They are like the worms who wriggle into the corners of the earth when it thunders, but when the storm passes, they again begin their destruction of the dirt again. All unconverted men are like this. You must be more than that. Are you more than devils? Do you believe further and better and beyond what devils believe? You say, "Oh yes, I am much more than the devils; for I believe that God exists, I behold my God in truth as he says in his word." But the Apostle, as does Isaiah, connects beholding God, knowing God, and faith in that God, by the life one leads as a result. Demons have no life of holiness; and what do you think about your own life? Is it answerable to your perception of the truth and the Savior? "What doth it profit, my brethren, though a man say he hath faith, and have not works? Can faith save him?" (James 2:14). The answer is, *No.* Such a system of belief may be found in devils. Oliver Heywood said, "If you know what a God he is, you would leap for joy, you would boast of him, and be transported with the manifestations of God, your God and exceeding joy."[27] A life that truly lives, lives in abundant life. "If faith without works is dead (James 2:14-26), then the Christian's grasp of truth is no stronger than its practice in love. Practice must flow from theory."[28] The end of hearing for the Christian is not chiefly to know and understand, but rather to believe, practice, and obey that which is taught; to hear and be up and doing. "O Zion, that bringest good tidings, get thee up into the high mountain; O Jerusalem, that bringest good tidings, lift up thy voice with strength; lift it up, be not afraid ... Behold your God!" You must behold him if you are ever to tell Judah to behold him. Where are you spiritually speaking? Are you on top of the high mountain, to praise with a voice of strength, without

---

[27] Heywood, Oliver, *The Works of Oliver Heywood,* Volume 4, (Edinburgh: John Vint, 1827) 14.
[28] Van Mastricht, Peter, *The Best Method of Preaching,* (Grand Rapids, MI: Reformation Heritage Books, 2013) 77.

worldly fear, where you *behold your God?* Where is the pitch of your voice in your praise to him or your prayers to him? Can you hardly be heard? Demons do not trust that such information about God is good, nor can they. They know it is true, but do not trust that it is *good;* their lives are not answerable to the truth of what they know. Believing is only the first step, for it must cultivate an assurance in you that Christ can carry you in his heart; you must be able to trust in the content of what you believe to be true about him and his work. Such a "looking" (beholding) is an act of the whole person trusting Christ and his sacrifice for sin by supernatural faith. This is to place trust in what one knows. "I will put my trust in him," (Heb. 2:13). It is very easy to *say* that God exists, to affirm *that word* you heard actually matters, to believe in his attributes, to believe in his love and compassion, but such words carry an empty sound when the experimental reality of your life indicates precisely the opposite, just as the demons do. You say one thing, and yet do something quite opposite to your creed. You say that you are a Christian, and you *behold God* in word only, where your life speaks something very different.

In this way, take heed to your profession of beholding God. Have high thoughts of God, and of his Christ, for we all must be very careful to take heed that we do not believe or entertain any error, any offensive thoughts of God, and profess his kingly dominion and highness as the one who exists and reigns. We must not believe anything that is contrary to his own revelation of himself. Such a belief, a wrong belief of God, can enslave men to fear, a fear of horror, which is the property of the devil. Devils believe and are full of horror, they shudder and cower even with the belief they have concerning God. But, "perfect love casteth out fear," (1 John 4:18). Christ's love for you will cast out such fear. Ungodly fear, will suppress all holy duties, and all true affection to God. It is the great art of the devil to possess men with the apprehension, if it is possible, that their life is the same as his own. If the devils can persuade a person, if they can persuade you, that God does not love you anymore, or that he does not love you today, that you are unreconcilable to God, or that you are too much of a sinner, just as they are, if they can make you believe this, just for a time, then it is a very easy thing for them to help keep you from the power of beholding God, the power of beholding the Christ, from ever having any good applied to your soul. The exhortation to *behold your God* is lost on the error of a denial of the truth of God's word. The fallen angels believe and tremble, believe, yet they are full of fear, terror and dread. They long to make you that way by stopping the words of the Savior from entering into your heart, soul and mind, or, warping and twisting what is already there so that it does you no good.

Behold your God as God so lays down in the word. Be at peace with God as he reveals himself, no matter what he tells you about who he is an what he does. Believe him when he testifies to his strong saving arm; his strong arm, not yours; trust that it is true. Believe him when he directs you to look to him and behold him in his being and attributes, trust that he is the Shepherd to you. He is the Shepherd who feeds you with knowledge and understanding. He is the one that carries you, and he does this through his sweet voice, the sound teaching of the Scripture. Believe him as if God was saying to you, "though you have often forgotten me, and though you have often turned down the wrong path, though you sin, not once a year or twice a year, or five times a year, but all the time, every day, missing the mark and feel so far away from me, yet, if you receive my Son, and if you receive the pardon I offer in and through him, if you come to me and repent, even if it is 70 times 7, you will be my friend, and you are adopted as my son or daughter, and you will behold me and you will know my comfort." Such a faith that holds *that* idea, is set in love to God, true affection and fellowship with him, one with another, as the Apostle John says. John Howe said, "For whatsoever thoughts tend to the making him unlovely, or not amiable in your eyes, have them far from you."[29] How can God be unlovely if properly understood and beheld in his word? The belief of atheists, hypocrites and demons are very cunning adversaries, and such thoughts will pull you away rather than bring you closer.

---

[29] Howe, John, *The Works of John Howe*, (New York: John P. Haykin, E. Sanderson, 1835), 677.

This makes the word of God a precious commodity to you. Yes, the light of nature is true and real, and to the regenerate, is a great blessing. There you behold your God in creation and see his providence everywhere; the heavens declare it too! (Psalm 19:1ff). But if you desire to attain the *mystery of godliness*,[30] if you are to believe the good tidings to any true foundation, this first principle that God exists must be squarely understood from the Scriptures, to behold him in his way. And this is why the character of God is so essential in your Christian walk. Although the world receives, through general revelation, a picture of God which is clear enough for them to acknowledge and seek after him, their fallen state is most quantifiably seen in rejecting him; most people reject God and reject his word. You must behold the one who can bring you near to God: behold the Christ at your table during the time you eat dinner, in eating, which is as it were a lively sermon, a daily pledge of the mercy of God in Christ to you; in *all* his provisions. Behold him in all your afflictions; all difficulties, all trials. Behold him in your most dangerous temptations. Behold him when you are well and in a time of prosperity. Behold him when you are sick, and by your entrance into the grave as God wills. Behold him in all the afflictions of your brethren, as though he himself were naked, hungry, and sick. Behold him in his covenant, in the crucified work and

---

[30] "And without controversy great is the mystery of godliness," (1 Tim. 3:16).

merit of King Jesus. Behold him born of a virgin, in his birth and incarnation. Behold him in his life and work. Behold him in his miracles. Behold him in his agony, and sweating drops of blood for you. Behold him in his curse for you, in shedding all his blood on the cross. Behold him as God's fellow, raised from the dead. Behold him in his exaltation and intercession to go between God and your soul. Behold even that the King cometh, and that quickly. There is nothing which so fully and clearly, so punctually and perfectly declares the mind of God in all particulars, which concern his existence and glory, his attributes and works, as the holy Scripture where Christ the King is beheld in all his glory. Want to know the mind of God? It's in the Bible. Want to know this great mystery of godliness as well? It's laid out to you in the Scriptures, in fact, in our very passage to behold him. Could any but God reveal it to us but by his Spirit? And since it is revealed in Scripture, do we not have great reason and evidence to believe that it was written by the finger of God? This is the way Christians view it, love it and cherish it. All spiritual good that is worked in us by the Spirit of God through Christ, to draw us to God, to behold him, is found in the Scriptures, he is beheld there and proclaimed from there. You must see Scripture to be written with God's finger, because no other than God could reveal such glorious truths to us about his Trinity, and his Son, and his cross, and his Spirit, and his love, and his grace and his will and his abundant life for his people in giving them a kingdom. Once we consider it, the rational soul comes to an unquestionable conclusion, that the Scripture is given by inspiration of God, because we find in it the only way of our access to, and acceptance with the God who is to be seen, beheld, and the only way of purifying us to have fellowship with this God, to have communion with him forever, is through his Son, through the revelation of his existence and will. Only God could teach us these things, which the minds of men or angels otherwise could never have conceived.

What does the word say, merely in our text, in the book of Isaiah about all this? This is where Paul looked when he commented on it in his letters and epistles; this is where the Apostles looked (the Old Testament was their bible). What does it say about him? "Behold, I will send my Messenger, and he shall prepare the way before me," *etc.* "Behold a voice cryeth in the wildernesses, Prepare you the way of the Lord, make strait in the desert a path for our God." "Behold every valley shall be exalted, and every Mountain shall be made low, and the crooked shall be straight, and the rough places plain," as the King comes in. "Behold the glory of the Lord shall be revealed, and all flesh shall see it together: for the mouth of the Lord hath spoken it." "Behold Zion, that bringest good tidings, get thee up into the high Mountains to proclaim its truth." "Behold O Jerusalem, that bringest good tidings, lift up thy voice with strength, lift it up, be not afraid;" worship him. "Behold, the Lord God will come with power, and his arm shall rule for him." "Behold, his reward is with him, and his work is before him." "Behold, the Lord says I will lay in Zion a Stone, a tried Stone, a precious Corner Stone," a sure foundation to all that believe and trust in him. "Behold, they shall call his name Immanuel:" which is by interpretation, *God with us;* to be observed and considered by those who have drawn near to him. "Behold, unto us a child is born, and unto us a Son is given, and the government is upon his shoulder." "Behold, and he shall be called by his name Wonderful, Counsellor, the Mighty God, the Everlasting Father, the Prince of Peace, the increase of his government and peace shall have no end." Behold I will give unto Jerusalem one that shall bring good tidings unto it." "Behold, this Redeemer shall come unto Zion; and unto them that turn from iniquity in Jacob, saith the Lord." *Behold your God.*

The first principle of the good news of the Gospel of God, is to *behold* the mighty God, that God exists and can be known through his Redeemer. In the next chapter we will consider the second principle of these good tidings, that God is man's Maker and has made him in his image.

Principle 2:
God Our Maker

"Sing, O barren, thou that didst not bear; break forth into singing, and cry aloud, thou that didst not travail with child: for more are the children of the desolate than the children of the married wife, saith the LORD. Enlarge the place of thy tent, and let them stretch forth the curtains of thine habitations: spare not, lengthen thy cords, and strengthen thy stakes; For thou shalt break forth on the right hand and on the left; and thy seed shall inherit the Gentiles, and make the desolate cities to be inhabited. Fear not; for thou shalt not be ashamed: neither be thou confounded; for thou shalt not be put to shame: for thou shalt forget the shame of thy youth, and shalt not remember the reproach of thy widowhood any more. For thy Maker is thine husband; the LORD of hosts is his name; and thy Redeemer the Holy One of Israel; The God of the whole earth shall he be called. For the LORD hath called thee as a woman forsaken and grieved in spirit, and a wife of youth, when thou wast refused, saith thy God. For a small moment have I forsaken thee; but with great mercies will I gather thee. In a little wrath I hid my face from thee for a moment; but with everlasting kindness will I have mercy on thee, saith the LORD thy Redeemer. For this is as the waters of Noah unto me: for as I have sworn that the waters of Noah should no more go over the earth; so have I sworn that I would not be wroth with thee, nor rebuke thee.

For the mountains shall depart, and the hills be removed; but my kindness shall not depart from thee, neither shall the covenant of my peace be removed, saith the LORD that hath mercy on thee," (Isaiah 54:1-10).

In Isaiah 54:1, there is found the picture of the barren woman, who complains of being abandoned by God. There are, here, in fact, many angles that could be unfolded within this passage. Being abandoned, feeling abandoned, is a most difficult providence. No one likes to be abandoned, especially as it relates to children. This idea is used metaphorically in light of these people.

In verse 2 this woman is challenged to expand on all sides to make room for her growing family. There is a great blessing in building the city back up again, and expanding it, to have people come to it. Not merely putting it back in the restoration to what it was, but furthering its borders to include *more* people. What a blessing in light of the initial abandonment! Verse 3 shows that growth will continue as her descendants move out into the villages and towns. When Judah's population went into exile leaving many of these villages and towns abandoned, the emptiness was filled by trespassers from neighboring areas. Now the people of God are coming back and reclaiming their land, even expanding it; they were initially feeling abandoned, but now they are revived.

In verses 4–5 Jerusalem is now to forget her helplessness, and exhorted to be bold in her understanding of God's relation to her as God's bride and God as her Maker. God, her Maker, is the one married to her (בעל), her owner as Maker and the one that causes her to grow as Husband. In this God protects, supports and nourishes her. He is *the Lord of Hosts* in this, a designation that revolves around God being the Lord of armies.[1] He is Protector, and Nurturer to them, as much as a Husband and Maker.

God is the Maker, the Lord of Hosts, the Husband, the Holy one of his church, the Redeemer of his people. He is the great King, the great providential sovereign who directs and guides all things for their good. God has *made* them, and as the God who made them he will *protect* them in every way possible. Even though they feel like they have been abandoned, God is there to redeem them, expand them, cultivate them, fight for them, in fact, he is married to them for he is not only their Maker but in fact their *very Husband.*

The heralding of the good news, the glad tidings of redemption, is the theme of all these *acts of love* as God uses the Persian kings (like Darius) to rebuild Jerusalem and reestablish the church in its home. *Yahweh of Hosts* was the title used for worship around the Ark of the Covenant in early Israel which was then transplanted to the Temple in Jerusalem. It recalls the Exodus, the wilderness journey, Joshua's conquest of

---

[1] The title itself "Lord of Hosts" is used over 200 times in the Bible, and its derivatives almost double that number. This is one of the largest collective descriptions of God in all Scripture, rivaling descriptions of God as *holy.*

Canaan, and David's conquest of the larger area of Palestine. God is the *God of war*, he is the Protector, as much as their Maker and Husband. The Holy One of Israel is the particular title used in Isaiah's earlier vision of Jesus Christ on the throne (Isaiah 6). It describes God as the one who is so lofty that the most insignificant parts of the vision of God, like the hem of his robe (seeing silver bells and pomegranates), are exceedingly glorious, and wholly other; he is unimaginable in his glory (Christ's service (bells) and sweetness (pomegranates) are in view there). This God links the church to the promise he made to Abraham by election, (Gen. 17:4-5; Romans 417-18), this God who would fight vehemently for his bride as a Husband. The God of the whole land, or the whole earth, shows that God owns all things.[2] He disposes of people and places and things as he sees fit. Would not the Creator, the maker of all men be able to do this? Would he not have leave to do this, to do that which he desires with his own?

In verses 6–8 the church, after having sinned and broken covenant with God, the God who is faithful, their maker, *renews* his marriage vows with them, and the broken marriage is healed. The feeling of being abandoned and the wrath of God against sin and wickedness, captivity, exile, are cast aside for *covenant renewal*. Though God forsakes them but for a little while, he will bring them back in mercy.

---

[2] "O LORD, how manifold are thy works! in wisdom hast thou made them all: the earth is full of thy riches," (Psa. 104:24).

In verses 9–10 God swears to his devotion. He refers back to his promise to Noah after the flood (Genesis 9:11) and maintains on the immutable oath of his devotion (חסד) and his everlasting covenant of peace with his people, he will save them; that covenant will not be moved.

In verse 5 he says, "For thy Maker is thine husband." This is the hinge on which this point turns. It may be more accurately translated, "For thy Husband is thy Maker." The verse is exegetical of the terms, "married wife" in verse 1, and "widowhood" in verse 4. "I," the prophet says, "have called thee married and widowed, thereby yoking thee to a husband, for thou hast a Husband, namely, thy Maker." This relationship of God in this *filial* way to his church is often asserted by the prophets. "Turn, O backsliding children, saith the LORD; for I am married unto you," (Jer. 3:14). "And I will betroth thee unto me for ever; yea, I will betroth thee unto me in righteousness, and in judgment, and in lovingkindness, and in mercies," (Hosea 2:19). "Draw me, we will run after thee: the king hath brought me into his chambers: we will be glad and rejoice in thee, we will remember thy love more than wine: the upright love thee," (Song of Songs 1:4). When this relationship is broken by his wayward people, *spiritual adultery* is the outcome. "Judah hath dealt treacherously, and an abomination is committed in Israel and in Jerusalem; for Judah hath profaned the holiness of the LORD which he loved, and hath married the daughter of a strange god,"

(Mal. 2:11). Idolatry itself is called "lewdness," "adultery," or "playing the whore." "Thy Redeemer" is the holy one who will not put up with such adultery. He is the God of the whole earth. "The earth is the LORD'S, and the fulness thereof; the world, and they that dwell therein," (Psa. 24:1). In terms of the physical earth, God is the maker, he is the God of the *whole* earth, not merely parts of it. Spiritually, though, from this time forth, he will be, "God of the whole earth," *morally* speaking, not only of the Jews, but also of the Gentiles; his husbandry will extend and does extend to them as he saves them. "Is he the God of the Jews only? is he not also of the Gentiles? Yes, of the Gentiles also," (Rom. 3:29). This section of Isaiah shows forth God as Maker, Husband, Lord of Hosts, Redeemer, Holy One, the God and King of all the earth. Amazing!

The doctrine that we will consider here is the second principle of the good tidings of the Gospel of God: that God is man's Maker and has made humankind in his image. This is not only clearly stated in the text, but also implied, in that God is man's maker, has made him a certain way, and all things attached both to making man and then redeeming man are given in verse 5. The image of God in man, how he is made, how man further ruins that image by spiritual adultery to her husband is the whole force of the passage. As God is man's Creator and Preserver, they derive from him their being, and the whole duration of their being throughout their life. God has a claim on all things that are created by him (which is everything). As long as people have *being* in this world, they are to live to his glory, for he is their maker. They should live to his glory, this is why he made them. Is there any part to the creation that is not assigned to God, for him, for all things are *for* him? "For it became him, for whom are all things, and by whom are all things," (Heb. 2:10). Menial things are ascribed to him, "For every beast of the forest is mine, and the cattle upon a thousand hills," (Psa. 50:10); cows are his, beasts of the forest like squirrels and moles, and hawks and mice and deer are his. He made and created everything, "And God saw every thing that he had made, and, behold, it was very good," (Gen. 1:31). What is out of his jurisdiction?

However, the great God is man's maker in a very *special* manner. He is his constant maintainer, owner, and provider of all they enjoy in a special relationship with him as rational beings. If there is a delight, if there is a comfort, if there is any help from him, all comes from God. If there is any pleasure in a fallen world, it is from the maker of all things even in light of the presence of evil. And as the maker of all men, and all things, he is the great disposer of all things being their maker. He has an indisputable right to dispose of his creation in any way he sees fit as the Great King. "Our God is in the heavens, he doth whatsoever he pleases;" and he does this with his own. "Know ye that the LORD he is God: it is he that hath made us, and not we ourselves; we are his people, and the sheep of his pasture," (Psa. 100:3). The bodies and souls, the material and immaterial parts of men are all God's work. "My substance was not hid from thee, when I was made in secret, and curiously wrought in the lowest parts of the earth," (Psa. 139:15). The Psalmist uses the word, "curiously wrought" which translates to *be squeezed or mixed* in a certain way, like colors of paint on a palate. God is the great Architect of man's constitution, the great Painter of the portrait of man. He places the immaterial inside the material in his creation, where he gives man the breath of God, the *nephesh* (breathing or breath) of the *neshamah*, the living being, who then has a soul.

God made man after his image: "And God said, Let us make man in our image, after our likeness: and let them have dominion over the fish of the sea, and over the fowl of the air, and over the cattle, and over all the earth, and over every creeping thing that creepeth upon the earth. So God created man in his own image, in the image of God created he him; male and female created he them. And God blessed them, and God said unto them, Be fruitful, and multiply, and replenish the earth, and subdue it: and have dominion over the fish of the sea, and over the fowl of the air, and over every living thing that moveth upon the earth," (Gen. 1:2628). Elohim, "God" fashions, "makes", man in his image and likeness. Man, *"adam"* is the crowing pinnacle of God's creation in the garden. He is created by divine counsel. He is placed in an exalted position because of this. He is given reign in a special place of God's choosing, in a garden which was to be extended over the face of the whole earth by his work before the glory of God. *Image* and *likeness* are synonymous words used to describe in what way man is a reflection of his maker. In no way is man God, but he is a *reflection* of God. Men look into a mirror and see a reflection of themselves. They raise their hand, and see a raised hand in the mirror; but they do not really see that hand in the mirror, for it is only a reflection of hand. These similes in English use *like* or *as* to refer to things in a *like nature*. Image and likeness refer to four things in which human beings who are created in God's image reflect him. Intellectual, moral, spiritual righteousness and holiness, as well as having an exercise of these things in dominion over the earth. "Let them have dominion (or rule) over the fish of the sea, over the birds of the air, and over the cattle, over all the earth and over every creeping thing that creeps on the earth," (Gen. 1:28). This is having dominion over God's creation as *vice-regent*. The word literally means "to tread" on them. As a lesser example, parents have God's commanded dominion over their children; they have been *given* dominion over their children. Many parents refuse to instruct and discipline their children, and when the children have not been disciplined, we find parents failing where God says they should be ruling, and what comes of it but chaos? Men have been given divine dominion, by divine right, over children, and in fact, over many things – over the whole earth. They are to reflect the God-quality of sovereignty by utilizing their spiritual, moral, and intellectual righteousness over creation for holy purposes. In so many ways men abuse creation instead of righteously ruling over it; and this is tragic, a result of the fall in them.

The 1647 Westminster Confession of Faith in 4:2 says it this way: "After God had made all other creatures, he created man, male and female, with reasonable and immortal souls, endued with knowledge, righteousness, and true holiness, after his own image, having the law of God written in their hearts, and power to fulfil it." That's also a key point, "righteous rule," for, ruling in holiness was Adam's responsibility. God wasn't going to do it for him. He gave Adam the power to fulfill dominion over the whole earth. "So God created man in his own image; in the image of God he created him; male and female he created them." Notice that the image of God is both made in male and female *together. They* are endowed with the image of their maker. The male is still given predominance in godly rule in the hierarchy of God's created order,[3] yet both male and female are created in this image to have spiritual, moral and intellectual righteousness before God and to use those God-given gifts to rule over creation and exercise human sovereignty; dominion reflecting the Great King. They are complimentary to one another in this as male and female.

---

[3] "But I would have you know, that the head of every man is Christ; and the head of the woman is the man; and the head of Christ is God," (1 Cor. 11:3).

These, "God blessed." The Maker blessed them, and that meant to endue with power for success, prosperity and longevity. Adam and Eve had everything they needed from God to fulfill the task that God had given them. This was to fulfill their station in God's covenant, and dominate the planet in knowledge, righteousness, and holiness. That would have reflected God's image in them to the world. In the beginning of this, Adam's labors did in its inception, look to fulfill God's task and rule creation. This is called the *cultural mandate*, "and God said to them, "Be fruitful and multiply; fill the earth."" "Bear fruit" by having dominion over the earth, by having children that as the prophet Malachi said, are *godly seed*. "That he might seek a godly seed," (Malachi 2:15); which is what God desires to be brought up as children to his elect people (to populate the earth and take dominion over it by godly seed). So here is found a divine aspect to procreation in that it partially fulfills the command which God had placed on them. That is the original intention of sexual intimacy, dominating the world in seed that is knowledgeable, righteous and holy with dominion. Unfortunately, in todays' culture the diamond of marital sex has been placed deeply into the mud. (This mandate has been lost in so many religious ways; but I do not wish to digress here on that issue).

This dominion that to be exercised, extended, "over the fish of the sea, over the birds of the air, and over every living thing that moves on the earth..." To "subdue" is related to "dominion and rule" of the former verse. It means "to bring into bondage" like *conquering* a nation. It is to serve by force. Adam was to take creation by force. He was to do this as if creation would not easily come under his rule, that it would take work. In this task Adam is exercising authority – human sovereignty, specifically given to him by his maker. Many times, the garden is thought about as if it were absolutely perfect in a "heavenly" kind of view, and there was no need to really do anything in it because at this point there was no fall. People tend to apply the idea of the final New Jerusalem to this initial paradise, where *work* was not needed. But this is not the case, in either of those places, in the garden, or in heaven. The garden was a sanctuary, the place where the Maker and the one made met together. But it was a *wild* place, where Adam and Eve were given abilities which empowered them for service, and by the blessing of God on them, they would be able to accomplish the task ... provided they held fast to being obedient to God in covenant with him. In the garden, they were to work.[4] And in living before him in this covenant, that God's will would be done on earth as it is done in heaven. The Maker "formed man of the dust of the ground, and breathed into his nostrils the breath of life; and man became a living being." Created by two essential ingredients, breath and clay (like the potter giving substance to the clay, which Isaiah speaks of in

---

[4] "Therefore the LORD God sent him forth from the garden of Eden, to till the ground from whence he was taken," (Gen. 3:23).

chapter 41 and 64) God formed man out of the mud of the ground. In his nostrils he breathed or blew into him life, and gave him a soul, *nephesh*. Literally, God the maker blew into him the "breath of lives" showing the multiplicity of man's makeup. In this breath, man becomes a living "soul" a whole man; material and immaterial brought together to make one being.

Man, being the pinnacle of creation, is given a prominent place, or the highest place, in the creative order. He is very special to God. There are no other created beings which are higher. Some may say the angels are higher as the Scriptures attest in Philippians 2, but this is the case *after* the fall of man and not before. God took special care and attention to make man in even conferring amidst the divine counsel when he was being made, "Let us make man in our image..." Unlike the rest of creation that he just spoke and made, mankind is special in this way.

God is man's Maker. Man has no reason to glory in himself. He has a derived being; his "self" is from his maker. Does a woman have beauty? Does a man have strength? Does a person have a keen mind? Does one have various endowments that give them special abilities? Why should such people glory in this? Are they not all God's creatures? Where did they get whatever it is that they have received? "Who maketh thee to differ?" (1 Cor. 4:7).

It is of the Maker that anyone is anything, excepting sin. And what, will man then glory in his sin?

It is a shame to him to defile this image. Will a man glory in his sin, where sin has taken away all his glory? God has formed man out of the clay, raised him from the very dust, clothed him with muscles, and skin and breathed into him the breath of life. He made him that was nothing, a mere pile of dust and mud, something, and gave him being.

God is the maker, the one who gives men being and *purpose*. The great God, whose chief end in all he does, is his own glory, it is because he is the first and best of beings.[5] He is man's maker, and made all men for his own pleasure. He has made man for himself, and man is to regard God as Maker, so that further along the lines that Isaiah preached, that God in light of the fall then may be seen as one's husband, the holy one, the Lord of Hosts, the Redeemer. One cannot see God for those further ideas without first seeing that God is man's maker.

Men have a simple test to see if they acknowledge in both theory and practice that God is Maker. It is often seen in a twofold way: the time they devote to him, and the glory they give him. To separate any part of their time from him, is to oppose his designs, and to try to endeavor to frustrate his supreme end, and sacrilegiously to rob him of his honor.

---

[5] *The 1647 Westminster Shorter Catechism* asks in Question 1. "What is the chief end of man?" (*i.e.*, what is man's purpose?) Answer, "Man's chief end is to glorify God, and to enjoy him forever," (Psa. 86:9; Isa. 60:21; Rom. 11:36; 1 Cor. 6:20; 10:31; Rev. 4:11; Psa. 16:5-11; 144:15; Isa. 12:2; Luke 2:10; Phil. 4:4; Rev. 21:3-4).

If men neglect or withhold any part of their time in service to God their maker, they hold his divine honor in contempt. It is due to his maker. But men fell, and they broke the covenant that God as Maker and Creator and Sovereign set up (we'll talk more about that in the next chapter). Even in this, it was the great sin of the church in Isaiah's time, of going after idols. Idolatry, at its root is self-love.[6] To set up self over their maker, to not do what man ought to do, and instead, do what is contrary which is idolatry. Man was created to work righteously and in holiness, not to be idle (idleness is a great sin, spoken of even in relationship to the wickedness of Sodom, which was burned with fire from the Lord because of it). Man is to serve his maker to God's glory,[7] not to steal service from him. Ministry, preaching, pastoral service, is *not* the only service given to God. Oftentimes that office is exalted as if all other stations in life are for some lesser end; as if it is the preacher's job to do all these religious things, and that man's job is just to acquiesce that the preacher ought to do them. But all of life is for service to God by all men, for even the light of nature teaches this. The proper end of life, is stolen from God when service is not rendered to the Creator by the creature. And when this happens, service is no longer

---

[6] "Mortify therefore your members which are upon the earth; fornication, uncleanness, inordinate affection, evil concupiscence, and covetousness, which is idolatry," (Col. 3:5).

[7] "I beseech you therefore, brethren, by the mercies of God, that ye present your bodies a living sacrifice, holy, acceptable unto God, which is your reasonable service," (Rom. 12:1).

given to God, but as a result of the fall, it is given to sin.[8] It is to take away a sacrifice from the altar of the Creator and Maker, and immediately offer it to the worst of idols, which is the self. How provoking is this to the Maker who made men? It's no wonder why God requires the whole succession of man's time to be devoted to his Maker. That whether they eat or drink, or whatever they do, they do all for the glory of God. Man's chief end is to glorify God in all things. And, all things should be done to his glory; making that the chief end of all their actions, "While I live will I praise the LORD: I will sing praises unto my God while I have any being," (Psa. 146:2), and this *in every way.*

Man's whole life is not to be squandered but redeemed. If God is man's Maker, then no time of their being as they exist and are upheld to, should ever be squandered. All their time is the property of their Creator. He is the Maker of men, and he has a right to every part of every second of every life. He wants men to squeeze out of the divine light of his word all glory in every act to his glorious name. He has a natural right to all of it, which is why the church is exhorted to *redeem the time.* Time is very precious (Eph. 5:16). Why? Because time is God's, and the creature owes his Maker *due glory in that time.* God will have his glory, and the Christian is to consider how they spend their time, and whether that time is glorious as one made in the image of God. Even the first fruits of time belong to God. As

---

[8] "...we should not serve sin," (Rom. 6:6).

man was made in God's image in knowledge, righteousness and holiness, the first day that man experienced was the Sabbath. Honor and respect were first given to God in this. There is a dedication of time that is first given to God, to serve the Author of man's being.[9] How do Christians, then, glorify their Maker? There is an example, of this, a perfect one.

Jesus Christ is the image of God, and this perfectly. Christ, in whom God is to be seen and beheld, is one who exemplifies the image of God in both his substance and glorious properties impeccably. Man is known as the image of God reflected. Christ is known as the image of God consubstantial with the Father. He is the image of God both in his essence and his substance. "Christ, who is the image of God," (2 Cor. 4:4). In his humanity he is perfect, in his divinity he is perfect. He upholds knowledge, righteousness and holiness, with dominion, perfectly.

Christ carried all dominion and perfect holiness in his person. In men, the image of God is *only accidental* respecting his quality; the church has a *mirrored* reflection. Christ is the actual image, in perfect dominion, in perfect knowledge, in perfect righteousness, in perfect holiness, without sin; and that unchangeably so. "...that God in all things may be glorified through Jesus Christ, to whom be praise and dominion for ever and ever. Amen," (1 Peter 4:11). "To the

---

[9] "...a wise man's heart discerneth both time and judgment," (Eccl. 8:5). "...the time is short," (1 Cor. 7:29).

only wise God our Savior, be glory and majesty, dominion and power, both now and ever. Amen," (Jude 1:25). "... hath put all things under his feet, and gave him to be the head over all things to the church," (Eph. 1:22).

Christ carried all authority and power as God's perfect image, which is why he is *full of grace and truth*, as the Apostle says (John 1:14). Man had authority and power, which by God's ordinance was seen in the garden, over creation by dominion. But even that is a faint reflection of what the Christ possesses. Christ is the image of God over his church, man is but a reflection of that. Christ looks to the bride to protect her and nourish her, and has all power to do so, has dominion over the whole world, the whole fall, to reverse it in men. Their lost image due to sin, the image they lost when Adam sinned, Christ alone can fix and redeem. He alone can protect her as the Lord of hosts, to redeem her as *the Redeemer*, to be holy for her as the Holy One, to be a husband to her to cultivate her qualities, but he is also her Maker, that created her and upholds her very being; though forsaken for a time, he makes the church his unblemished wife. "Come hither, I will shew thee the bride, the Lamb's wife," (Rev. 21:9). Christ, "Who being the brightness of his glory, and the express image of his person, and upholding all things by the word of his power, when he had by himself purged our sins, sat down on the right hand of the Majesty on high," (Heb. 1:3). He rules and reigns for them on his glorious throne in knowledge, righteousness and holiness, with dominion as the great King; he gives them a kingdom.[10]

God's image is in both man and Christ. In man it is by creation; and so it is in all men even the worst men, though fallen, in as much as there is in them an aptitude to know and conceive of God, though they suppress this truth in unrighteousness unless they are created anew. But they conceive of God imperfectly because the image of God is marred and depraved due to the fall. Instead of glorifying God, they despise him. It can then only be a by similitude of glory that they reflect God's image back to him in knowledge, righteousness and holiness; they must be renewed, recreated by their Maker who restores the fallen image. In heaven, even, they will resemble God's glory, and yet, still, only reflect it.

Christ is the flawless image of God. Jesus Christ not only is exactly in the image of God, but in the most proper sense *is* the image *of the Father.* And as the great archetype of God, the exact image of God, he knows what that image should be and could be in now, fallen men; man's *potential* is known by him most intimately. He is the image of God in operation, because it is he that renews and works God's image in fallen men by the power of the Spirit. He renews them by a new act of creation (John 3:1-10). He renews them *by* the power of his Spirit. He re-creates them as their spiritual Maker. He creates them *again* and remakes them *again.* In fact,

---

[10] "Fear not, little flock; for it is your Father's good pleasure to give you the kingdom," (Luke 12:32).

Jesus calls this in John 3 being born *again*. He is the image of God in communication, as he appeared as the Logos of God to the fathers in the Old Testament, and disciples in the New Testament. He is the image of God in its essence, in a communicative property of revealing the Maker of all things and declaring his substance both in teaching it and being it. He knows what men can be, and how glorious they can reflect the Creator, even as Adam did in the garden before the fall, even *more so* by his Spirit. He is the image of God in his person; and that in both natures, both as God and Man he is perfectly God's image. For, the most perfect image of God is, Christ the Lord who is the perfect image of what holiness and righteousness look like, as the God-man. He is the perfect image of God because he is God, "... equal with God," (Phil. 2:6). He is God's image infinitely, perfectly resembling and declaring the Father (John 1:18).

Christ is also the image of God as he is Man. "God was *manifest* in the flesh," (1 Tim. 3:16). Being manifest in the flesh, this was the God-head dwelling in Christ bodily; in respect of the unutterable presence of the divine nature in him as being *fully God.*

This is also seen by Christ's miracles, for in those works he manifested his divine nature, and showed God in the world as one declaring the Father and working by the Spirit *without measure.* In his human nature he alone is qualified with knowledge, righteousness, and holiness, along with all other gifts of the Spirit without measure in this way. For if man is God's image in respect of these three things, knowledge, righteousness and holiness, Christ is so much more being God himself.

Christ, then, as he is God, is not only the image of the *invisible* God, but as man, he is the *visible* image of the invisible God. Who is more fit, then, "to restore the image of the Father lost in men, then he that was the eternal image of the Father? Who is more fit to break open the fountain of God's love, then he that was the Son of his love? The personal word became the enunciated word, to declare to men his Father's nature and will: he that is the middle person in the Trinity, is fittest to be the middle man, or mediator between God and man."[11] Christ stands gleaming as the perfect image of God in between fallen man with his marred image, and God with his holy image that is of consuming fire, and can make the two meet, because he changes men into new beings to join them to God's holiness without fear of ever being consumed (Hebrews 12:29).

This is Isaiah's point, that Christ, man's Maker, the true image bearer, restores the fallen image of man who was originally created in knowledge, righteous and holiness. Man did not climb out of the primordial ooze by way of some evolution (one of the most absurd and ridiculous lies the devil ever introduced into the darkened mind of man which darkened minds believe as

---

[11] Byfield, Nicholas, *An Exposition Upon the Epistle to the Colossians*, (London: T. Snodham. and Edward Griffin for Nathaniel Butter, 1615) 35-36.

a substitute to the truth of God's dominion). Man was created by God *from* the dust of the ground. The difference between the heathen conception of man and the Christian conception of man is that the heathen believe man is *just dust* from the ground. But God breathed into man the breath of life and made him in his image. This is a fundamental principle to the good news. There is a God, and this God is man's Maker who made man in his image.

Reader, your Maker is your Husband if you are a believer. People often think that just because God made men that all people are God's children; are we not all his offspring? (Acts 17:28-29). But God has a very particular definition of *sons and daughters,* and that definition is not merely *offspring* as referring to Creator and creature.[12] That God is your Maker as a Christian, true enough, and so, the Author of all your blessings. This point is necessary to the good news. It is necessary for you to understand it as such, because good tidings of comfort from God, houses in it the worship due to our Maker in prayer, praise, and adoration being made in his image. You submit to God as Maker in prayer seeking his will. But you praise your Maker as both Maker and Redeemer in your adoration of him. You adore all the attributes of this God through Christ, as the Maker of heaven and earth but then ... he takes your fallen image,

---

[12] *The 1647 Westminster Shorter Catechism* in Question 34 asks, "What is adoption?" Answer, "Adoption is an act of God's free grace, whereby we are received into the number, and have a right to all the privileges, of the sons of God," (1 John 1:12, 3:1; Rom. 8:17).

restores it by a spiritual operation through the power of his finite Spirit, takes up residence in you, and such a renovation of that image makes you a new creature. You are made a new creation ... all over again (2 Cor. 5:17; Gal. 6:15). If God alone is able to perform this mighty work of renewing your image in recreating it for his glory in Christ Jesus as Redeemer, then as *Husband* to you, and that God is willing to do it, this is a great cause for your happiness. You look to his work to glorify your Maker not only by creation, but by *recreation*. Your Maker turns to be your Husband. He never ceases being your Maker, but how sweet is it that Christ makes you his bride, and he now becomes your Husband, to have such concern for you? Paradise lost is now paradise *fully* restored, newly renovated, and so much more. "And Jesus said unto him, Verily I say unto thee, Today shalt thou be with me in paradise," (Luke 23:43). The penitent thief hanging on the cross with him, in a most deplorable situation, dying there, and yet, avowing that Christ is King and Lord and has a kingdom, a *restorating kingdom* in which this fellow wanted to be remembered by the Great King, is a remarkable testimony to his recreation by the Spirit. What are you as a man or woman, a fallen man or woman, that God should be mindful of you, to remember you when as he is Maker and Redeemer and has come into his Kingdom? And who are you as part of the mass of fallen humanity in Adam, that your Maker should visit with you to fix you to draw near to you and you to him as a Husband who brings in his wife into his banqueting house, where the banner over her is love? (Song of Songs 2:4). What great grace has the great Maker manifested to you, that when you had forfeited all the blessings to be expected of him as your Creator, in rebelliously casting off that holy image, that natural obligation you were under to obey him, he should redeem you as the Redeemer as your husband and Savior? What is this that he would take notice to make *you new?* What an amazing recreation of the image of God in you. If you believe and trust in him that he can do it, no longer will you feel abandoned like, "a woman forsaken," for he does not cast you off. He does not merely vindicate himself on you. He does not render you miserable, and treat you as an enemy, but rather, he recreates your fallen humanity, he reverses the fall in you, the entirety of your fallen humanity, body and soul, and makes you an object of his favor that you might come boldly before his throne, to gaze even on the most insignificant parts (the hem of his High Priestly garment) of his glory as wonderous in Jesus Christ as the Great King on his throne. "For thy Maker has now *become* your husband." What has he done in this but preserve you, exercising patience and long-suffering towards you, lavishing on you favors, health, homes, family, children, friends, and then, yet, in Christ, he opens up to you a new and living way that you might return to him in this renewed image to enthrone him in your praises. He sets out the eternal covenant in the cross of Christ to you, and shows you his terms of peace and reconciliation, and that by the blood of Jesus, he renews you in the spirit of your mind by his everlasting covenant. He makes of you a brand-new creature. What you were not before, where that blackened image worked all kinds of foul things before him as a pitiful creature, he makes that image thrive in you by the power of his Spirit. He renews you after a renewed image, after the image of Christ conformed to his likeness. That in that renewing, you might be entitled to all those blessings lost in the garden, and then have your delight improved by being secured by your Maker in a new and nearer relation to God through Christ by the power of the Spirit as your husband. In the garden it was but one sin and all is lost. In the wedding chamber Christ refreshes you with all his benefits and makes you lovesick for his work, and his merit, and his security. In this, the Maker of heaven and earth treats those that are in this way reconciled to him by the blood of his Son, not only as his creatures but as his adopted children. This is why we sing from the Psalter:

Let Isr'el in his Maker joy,
and to him praises sing:
Let all that Zion's children are,
be joyful in their King, (Psalter, 149:2)

And since his one and only Son whom he has appointed heir of all things, is not ashamed to call *you* brethren, what does he do but treat you, now, as joint heirs with

77

him, and beckons you to call God your Father, in fact to call him Husband. What kind of considerations should be made here, that God our Maker, God our Redeemer, the Lord of Hosts, God of all the earth, the Husband of the church, should be served in these images that he has made, and now made anew by his Spirit?

I'll exhort you that it is reasonable for you to *serve* such a Maker and Husband all the days of your life. Is it reasonable to listen to him at his word? That is a service to him. Is it reasonable to live before him all the days of your life to love him in sincerity? That is a service to him. Is it reasonable that you set down a full reformation of life before him? That is a service to him. Is it reasonable that you do all to glorify him who could have left you in the mass of perdition? That is a service to him. Is it very unreasonable to sin against his designations both as Maker and Redeemer? It is reasonable to conclude that he is to be earnestly pursued because he is so infinitely gracious in Christ as both Maker and Husband? He is so liberal, that God will *give his Holy Spirit* to those that ask him. He is so liberal that he will give grace and spiritual life to those that seek him while he can be found. He is so liberal that he hands you his very *Kingdom* to live in. He is not standing over you with a club to beat you down, but gives you the greatest motive and encouragement to holy service in the power of his Son, the Christ, by taking that black and sinful image and renewing it in knowledge, righteousness and holiness with godly dominion. Did you know that you will even rule and reign with him in his kingdom? (2 Tim. 2:12; Rev. 20:6). He delivers a kingdom to you, that you would sit with him on his throne to rule and reign. This is godly dominion, which answers directly to a renewed image in you by the work of the Christ who is Maker and Husband.

If God is the sovereign Disposer of our being, because this is a necessary consequence of that relation of our Maker to us, he is our Creator, it should move you to consider that you quickly turn, in all your ways to be serviceable to him; to consecrate your whole life to service to the Great King. Since God is our Maker, and since he is the Sovereign God over all the earth, (is this not Isaiah's plea?), seeing he is the Author of your being, since he has a right to its sovereign disposal in whatever way he sees fit, would it not be in your best interest to improve the image of God in you, to conform to Christ's image for the glory of God day by day by day? Those who reject this idea, and reject this Christ, what horrible times can they expect, having their lives filled with pain and their futures filled with the same, even into eternity? Two thieves died on crosses next to Christ but only one went to into paradise with him. It is a most horrible thing at the end to fall into the hands of the Living God,[13] who, as he has made us, knows how to punish us for our disobedience with all the kinds and degrees of torment if we reject him! Our souls should be excited, ravished

---

[13] "It is a fearful thing to fall into the hands of the living God," (Heb. 10:31).

with delight, seeking pleasures at his right hand forevermore, look to his right hand, his hand of power and grace in the Christ. Our Maker knows how to excite our souls in this. Where is joy and happiness to be found? God is able, as Maker and Husband of the redeemed, to renew that image in such a way as to make life now wonderful, and everlasting life beautiful, with words that are described as Paradise. What begins here will continue in fullness there: *For thy Maker is thine husband,* and God as husband never forsakes his people, for he will never drive away poor sinners away that come to him to be renewed. To consider our Maker, as creatures, we should constantly have a view to the love of the husband to the church, to have the bridegroom be our Maker and Redeemer and Protector, and all things to us. Only he can enliven our souls with such rapturous joy, why would the Christian not seek and desire to entertain that notion all his days?

And if you have not had this Christ remake you, it is with the hand of faith that you can take hold of him. Faith is the hand of the soul, it takes hold of that mercy which God has provided for us in Christ Jesus, "with everlasting kindness will I have mercy on thee, saith the LORD thy Redeemer," (Isa. 54:8). And yet you might say, I have far too many sins, and I am too much of a sinner for Christ to accept me like a husband to a wife. Where did you learn that? Where did Christ ever say that to you? You are very afflicted if you think that way. Nowhere in the Scriptures is there any reason to think in that way. Christ says, "O thou afflicted," yes, you sinner, who are afflicted with such thoughts, "tossed with tempest, and not comforted, behold, (*he says*) I will lay thy stones with fair colours, and lay thy foundations with sapphires," (Isa. 54:11). He says he is very rich and liberal to you in mercy. He says reach out by faith and believe that such a One who Made you, can remake you, for your sins are not bigger than he is a Savior. You can never out-sin his grace.

Consider that respecting God's image in men respects the Maker of that image. Renewed image bearers know that sin defaces the image of God. I have dealt with this extensively in a work that I did concerning Joseph, so I am not going to rehash all that exegetical work here.[14] But if you are a Christian, you know that sin is very ruinous to the image of God in men. It is then very important for you to cultivate those things that surround knowledge, righteousness and holiness, and that cast-off sin, to the glory of Christ who has Redeemed you from it. Redeem the time, see time as precious, because your Maker has given you a limited amount of it to use for his glory. Be a shining image bearer. For the idea of the image bearer that glorifies God enters into a whole host of places practically and theologically, such as the origin of life and the dignity of human life, which has far reaching applications. For example, renewed image bearers know that killing

---

[14] See my work, *Joseph's Resolve, the Unreasonableness of Sinning Against God.*

God's image is a capital offense. Capital offenses in the Maker's law deserve capital punishment, because God has a very high view of life, not a low one. This has consequences on murder, on abortion, euthanasia, on foul speech against others, on reputation, on all kinds of aspects tied to man being made in God's image, which is to be honored.

Renewed image bearers know that both men and women bear the image of God in them. Women as individuals are to be respected and there was no one in the world that more highly praised and respected women than the Christ, just read his Gospels. They are image bearers of their Maker and are to be treated very highly as such. Both men and women have specific roles and those specific roles are ordained of God. This affects transgender ideas, cross dressing, just the appearance of a person in their choice of clothing and such, their self-identification; all these issues fall into this idea of the Maker's prescription for holiness since people are his image bearers. They will either choose to sin in this, or they will choose to uphold God's prescriptions. Man's God-ordained image in knowledge, righteousness and holiness comes directly into play here.

Renewed image bearers (Christians) know that creation is to be dominated by those who have a renewed image of God in them. This has far reaching implications on how one treats the environment. Today men and women worship nature, instead of dominating it as image bearers. They want to kill the children but save the trees. They have a radically warped sense of what their Maker requires of them and what it means to dominate the earth. This, further, has far reaching applications to art, music, aesthetics, creativity, and how all those are used for the Maker's glory.

Renewed image bearers know that injustice is evil. All kinds of injustice refer to rejecting the Maker of men, by mistreating his image bearers, and ignoring his instructions for redemption, life and godliness. Where God is not respected, it is inevitable that his image-bearers will also suffer a loss of respect.

Renewed image bearers know that speech is to be controlled and tamed to never slander. "Therewith bless we God, even the Father; and therewith curse we men, which are made after the similitude of God. Out of the same mouth proceedeth blessing and cursing. My brethren, these things ought not so to be," (James 3:9-10). All things concerning truth and speech revolve around this idea of reflecting God's image. God's image-bearers can think God's thoughts after him as they hold to his authorized truth and knowledge from the speech communicated by their Maker to them both reading the word, but especially in hearing the word preached to them.

If the image of God is defaced in such a horrible way, if it is marred, if it is depraved, cursed and fallen, men are unable to do anything that God requires of them as their Maker now that the curse is set upon them; this poses a great problem. They become rebels, atheists, fools, godless heathen, pagans, wayward, abominable, filthy, unrighteous, unholy, transgressors in all things; just to name a few biblical derivations of what God's Spirit has written down concerning them. This idea is what we will study next, the third principle being that in the fall, the image of God in man, was subject to the curse and made as black as the blackest darkness; that which was made by God as a reflection of his excellence, was befouled, made filthy, perverted, debased, by just one sin, Adam's original sin in the garden.

Principle 3:
The Curse of God on Man

"The earth also is defiled under the inhabitants thereof; because they have transgressed the laws, changed the ordinance, broken the everlasting covenant. Therefore hath the curse devoured the earth, and they that dwell therein are desolate: therefore the inhabitants of the earth are burned, and few men left," (Isaiah 24:5-6).

We find in this passage a prophecy of Isaiah concerning God's coming judgment. It is because, "the earth also is defiled under the inhabitants thereof." "Defile," as a word used in this text, is only mentioned twice in Scripture; it's very precise in its use (also found in Numbers 35:33).[1] But the effect of it is everywhere seen. The ground האדמה and land הארץ are cursed because of men, and there is blood that has soaked into it; it is *defiled.* Compare Genesis 3:17 in which the ground האדמה is cursed because of Adam. Then, in Genesis 4:10–12 Cain, who had been a tiller of the ground האדמה, must flee to the land ארץ or "the city" of the land (Gen. 4:10) because he spilled his brother's blood on the ground and defiled it; the defiled land is where Abel's blood cries out. The inhabitants of this land in Isaiah

---

[1] "So ye shall not pollute the land wherein ye are: for blood it defileth the land: and the land cannot be cleansed of the blood that is shed therein, but by the blood of him that shed it," (Num. 35:33).

have been devastated by defilement, or as Jeremiah 23[2] uses the term, *profaneness*. Why are they *profane*, and why are they *defiled?* Why is the ground soaked with blood? Why is sin so infectious and *so far reaching?*

Isaiah answers this question by saying, "because they have transgressed the laws, changed the ordinance, broken the everlasting covenant." These are the reasons for the coming destruction of God's judgment on the inhabitants of the land.[3] They are law-*less*, have rejected God's prescription for holiness, and they have broken the everlasting covenant. These inhabitants of the land, are morally bankrupt. They have substituted what God requires of them, and are doing what they want, in a law-*less* way (and yes, I'm italicizing the "less" part of *lawless* because they are rejecting God's commandments, his law, and are without his law, in this way), which in turn shows they have broken, in their sin, the everlasting covenant. What happens to a land that is filled with law-*less-ness?* These people are covenant breakers, and laws are contained in God's covenants, both the laws and covenant, contain stipulations where *curses* shall fall on those who break them; this is a very simple covenantal idea and present in all God's covenants with men. "Therefore hath the

---

[2] "For the land is full of adulterers; for because of swearing the land mourneth; the pleasant places of the wilderness are dried up, and their course is evil, and their force is not right. For both prophet and priest are profane; yea, in my house have I found their wickedness, saith the LORD," (Jer. 23:10-11).

[3] See my work, *Christ Commanding His Coronavirus to Covenant Breakers,* for a modern-day application of this prophetic idea.

curse devoured the earth, and they that dwell therein are desolate." A permanent covenant (on God's side) that is broken by defiling men (on a sinner's side) because of a curse, or literally, the oath of God against this, is Isaiah's point here. The cursing of God is a further judgment as a result of a broken covenant and a sin ridden land, one in which blood is soaked down into the very soil and has defiled it. The curse is unleashed, and once it is unleashed it continues without limit until judgment is brought by God against sin and wickedness; and the infinite need of satisfaction to God's justice must be met. The word "desolate" אשם (*asham*) shows that these wicked people are branded with the dreadful curse of God for breaking the everlasting covenant. Better yet, they are utterly *contaminated* by sin. That word "contamination" is an excellent picture word in this way. Even the *church* is responsible for some of the land's guilt in all this because they too have contributed to idolatry, contaminating everything by sin, not following God's prescription and are partakers of the *defiling* nature of the curse.

Isaiah then says, "...therefore the inhabitants of the earth are burned, and few men left," (Isa. 24:5-6). Is it not interesting that *fire* is used as the outcome of judgment against sin, that the land will be *scorched?* "But the heavens and the earth, which are now, by the same word are kept in store, reserved unto fire against the day of judgment and perdition of ungodly men," (2 Peter 3:7). "Looking for and hasting unto the coming of the day of God, wherein the heavens being on fire shall be dissolved, and the elements shall melt with fervent heat?" (2 Peter 3:12). Isaiah, in his text, takes Hosea's *covenant breach,* which Isaiah would have known about, and applies it to the earth, the land, the inhabitants, in this prophesy of God's judgment. Hosea said, "But they like men have transgressed the covenant: there have they dealt treacherously against me," (Hosea 6:7). Like "*A-dam*" they have transgressed the covenant. *Do this and live*, and so, they *did not do this* and instead enacted spiritual adultery over and over again, forcing God out of the sanctuary, defiling his worship, and breaking his laws *as covenant breakers like Adam*. Isaiah makes this curse more inclusive, "The *earth* is polluted because of its inhabitants, who have transgressed laws, violated statutes, broken the ancient covenant (*berit 'olam*)" (Isa. 24:5). The phrase *berit 'olam* "ancient" or "eternal" or "everlasting" covenant is applied to all the covenants throughout the Scriptures; the Noahic covenant (Gen. 9:16), Abrahamic covenant (Psa. 105:9-10), Mosaic covenant (Lev. 24:8), Davidic covenant (2 Sam. 23:5) ...and the New Covenant (Isa. 55:3; 61:8). In these the church is referenced. But make note, Isaiah's judgment in his prophesy is directed to *all* the nations (which includes the church), which shows that this use of the phrase is not part of the church's covenants (exclusively), but is linked to the *earth*, all the inhabitants of the earth, and has a direct reference to the inhabitants of the earth breaking God's statues, laws,

breaking *the covenant made with all men.* When did
this happen? When did all the earth break covenant
with God? This use in Isaiah is not a reference to the
covenant of *grace,* of Noah, Abraham, Moses, David, *etc.*
It is a reference to the covenant with *Adam.* It is a
reference to the broken everlasting *Covenant of Works*
that one is born under, as guilty, lawless, covenant
breaking defilers, in fact, that which contaminates all
men all over the earth; and God says, judgment is coming
upon them because of it, (*cf.* John 8:43; Matthew 13:14; 1
Cor. 2:14).

Consider, then, in light of this, the third
principle of the good news, which teaches *the bad news*
that all men have sinned in Adam, are defiled, and under
the curse of God. One cannot have the good news
without understanding the bad news. Good news
implies that there *is* bad news. God exists, principle 1,
God created Adam in knowledge, righteousness and
holiness, and he was to take dominion, making the
garden prosper across the face of the earth as one made
in God's image, principle 2. But now, principle 3,
whatever Adam was to do in the garden, it refers to holy
and spiritual service of the Lord, as commanded by God,
which he failed in and the curse of that failure fell on all
men. Adam was priest of the garden, the garden being
the sanctuary of God, the place where Adam drew near
to God and walked with God (Gen. 3:8). The covenant
that God placed Adam in was not an option for him. The
instruction God gave him was a command, summarized

in, "do this and live," (Gen. 2:17). It concerned life or death for good or evil for Adam and all his posterity. "And the LORD God commanded the man, saying, Of every tree of the garden thou mayest freely eat: But of the tree of the knowledge of good and evil, thou shalt not eat of it: for in the day that thou eatest thereof thou shalt surely die," (Gen. 2:16-17). In principle 3, all men are defiled in Adam.

There are three elements of this covenant that defile men. [1] A promise of eternal life. If Adam had, as one exercising knowledge, righteousness and holiness in the right way, exercising holy dominion, the law of God, he would have merited eternal life. Paul even comments on this, "And the commandment, which was ordained to life," (Rom. 7:10) ... it now brings death. The law of God's covenant, do this and live, now brings death because Adam decided he wanted to take a shortcut to holiness, and get there that much quicker. What is the least work and quickest way to do what God says but in my own way, for my own agenda, to do what I think is important? This is man's constant dilemma and sin. [2] There was the prescription of the conditions for obtaining the promise. "Don't eat of the tree." And also, [3] the penal sanction against transgressors of the conditions of the covenant; break the law and you get punished. "Dying you shall die." God requires the complete sanctification of the parties involved in the covenant or he threatens punishment. The penal sanction is death (Gen. 2:17). Death (both spiritual and physical) is the consequence of sin and, therefore, not natural for man. The rebellious and disobedient will procure death, earn *by* their cursed wages, cursing, fire, burning, as Isaiah mentions. For Adam, death will follow *as a consequence of eating the forbidden tree.* For men, death will follow as a consequence of eating the forbidden tree *in Adam.*[4]

The sacrament of the tree of knowledge of good and evil signified the promise of the covenant. There is a sealing of the covenant in the sign of the tree. But it also signifies the curse of the covenant. When a man partakes of any of the sacraments, he comes under two conditions in the covenant: 1) an oath and 2) a curse, and makes himself liable to punishment if he deals treacherously with God. This is why Paul warns Christians to examine themselves to be sure they do not abuse the sacrament when they eat (as an example of this in the church today) of the sacrament of the Supper (1 Cor. 11). In eating it, one places one's self either under blessing or cursing.

Adam will be punished and die if he eats of the tree. The term *death* is used generally here to include spiritual and physical death. Death surrounds everything that this penal sanction, that this just declaration, pronounces. This is spoken to Adam as the head of mankind, as covenant head, as federal head, as *representative* on behalf of all men. Physical and spiritual death on behalf of all men is the outcome of his

---

[4] "For as in Adam all die," (1 Cor. 15:22).

disobedience. And this stipulation God placed on Adam against such a breach would be administered immediately upon his disobedience. And the moment he finished his sin in eating the fruit, he felt the change, and it began immediately.

Consider, there are various meanings of death in Scripture. Simply, death is the separation of body and soul. The soul becomes *unfit* for the body. Genesis 3:19, "For dust you are, and to dust you shall return." When the bible speaks about the body as dust, it is always negative. Abraham (Gen. 18:27) says he is dust and ashes. David (Psalm 103:14) says that God knows our frame (Gen. 8:21 an *evil* frame) as dust. The serpent is said to have dust as its food in crawling and slithering on its belly after the curse showing forth the angelic submission of the devil to God's created order as least because he is wicked (Gen. 3:14). In Isaiah 65:25, *dust* is the sinful flesh. *Death* means vanity or frustration of this life along with all its pains and miseries. Death represents everything opposite to happiness. Death, spiritual death, is given in Ephesians 4:18, "having their understanding darkened, being alienated from the life of God." In Eph. 2:1, men are those, "who were dead in trespasses and sins."

Death also refers to the terrors of an evil conscience. In hell sinners will one day rejoin their body in everlasting destruction by the wrath of God on them for their wickedness.[5] This torment will last forever. It is a punishment that is eternal. Matthew 25:46 says, "And these will go away into everlasting punishment." Mark 9:44 states, "...where, "Their worm does not die, And the fire is not quenched."" All the actions and thoughts of every person shall be tried in the judgment, and those not under the blood of Christ shall be eternally damned, to live a perpetual existence of death forever.

Death is certainly terrible, but a further *cursing* on sin is absolutely necessary due to God's promise to enact justice on it. The curse is based on the majesty of God, who is a jealous God for his own glory. Exodus 34:14, "For you shall worship no other god, for the LORD, whose name is Jealous, is a jealous God." God cannot deny himself; he cannot deny his supreme majesty. 2 Timothy 2:13 says, "...he cannot deny himself." He must punish wickedness because he is holy. A holy God cannot be peaceably joined with a sinner without satisfaction made to his justice. Someone *must* pay for treachery against breaking his covenant, and sinning against his character. Eternal death is not a random decision. It is set and constituted on the holy nature of God. Job 33:12–13 says, "For God is greater than man. Why do you contend with Him?" He is just and holy as his law is just and holy and will not allow it to be broken

---

[5] James explains that to the conscience, material possession which pulled people away from Christ will be a witness against them in hell under judgment, "Your gold and silver is cankered; and the rust of them shall be a witness against you, and shall eat your flesh as it were fire," (James 5:3).

without righteous repercussions. There is no contending with him.

The promise made to Adam in the garden was eternal life, but Adam broke God's law and forfeited it. Now, many Christians misunderstand the nature of the law and think the *moral law* is intrinsically bad. They think that the Law (*i.e.* the Ten Commandments) only brings death and that it was *designed* to bring death and today many professing Christians want no part of that. And then they quote Galatians 3:21, "For if there had been a law given which could have given life, truly righteousness would have been by the law." But, it is not that the Law created death, it merely points out the relation that people have to the law as it reflects God's character. It is only *death* to *those* who are *fallen* in Adam and have *darkened minds*. God *upholds* his own law and he does not die. God *keeps* his own law and does not die. The saints and angels in heaven *do God's will perfectly*, "thy will be done ... as it is in heaven," and they do not die, which is as keeping of the law. God is holy, and his law points to his holiness. The law is a curse to those who are fallen, and without Christ, because it damns them in light of God's holy character. Where there is no covering (no atonement), the law stands in full light to the relationship of that soul to God. The law condemns that soul because that soul is imperfect, and

God requires *perfection*.[6] This in and of itself destroys the idea of, "I'm not as a bad the next guy," theology. It is true that the sentence of condemnation will be to the letter of the law for each person who has sinned against God. But the idea of the curse, and the breaking of God's covenant is about being imperfect, which is the real problem.

This broken covenant is mentioned or seen in almost every chapter of Scripture in some respect. The fallen condition of man is focused in almost every chapter of the bible. Why is this? It is because Adam affected all men for all time in his original sin and fall and made them all imperfect. Romans 5:12, "Therefore, just as sin came into the world through one man, and death through sin, and so death spread to all men because all sinned." What Adam broke, is called the *Covenant of Works*. In the idea of "works," a Covenant of Works, God manifests himself as supreme Lawgiver and chief good desiring to make man a partaker of his eternal happiness *if he would obey*. God desires men to be holy, and if they are holy they will be happy because they will be *like* him. But Adam listened to that angel of light, the devil, that crafty serpent, the dragon, took a shortcut to holiness, thinking he could get there, on the advice of the seraphic angel being tempted in the garden, and believed there was a faster, easier, way to holiness than God's

---

[6] "Thou shalt be perfect with the LORD thy God," (Deut. 18:13). And Jesus said, "Be ye therefore perfect, even as your Father which is in heaven is perfect," (Matt. 5:48).

method. That sounded good to him, to be like God *quicker*, so he broke the covenant by disobeying God in the one thing that God told him not to do. This was the same sin of the devil, who fell as a result of *pride*, (Isa. 14:12-13). It is always the same thought process when sin enters the heart – my way is better than God's way.

In this covenant, Adam had no mediator. Adam was on his own; *he* was the representative for all men. The promise of life to be obtained in the *Covenant of Works* would have been gained by continued good works, good merit. He would have worked for a reward by debt.[7] It is why this part of Adam's time in the garden is often referred to *his probation*. This Covenant of Works conditioned eternal life if Adam would obey. Adam was required to uphold the character of God's person in the law reflecting God's glory *perfectly*. He may have certainly done this for a time, but did not ultimately do it for all time, (which was required in that covenant). After that *one single act of sin*, Adam fell, and all men fell with him, all were placed under the curse.

What was the fall's effect on mankind? The fall of Adam brought death to himself, death to all men, and brought in the death of Christ. The covenant was made with Adam, not only for himself, but for his posterity, all mankind, descending from him by ordinary generation, sinned in him, and fell with him, in his first transgression. Death to himself and all men was its

---

[7] When I say "by debt" that means that God would have *owed* him something had he kept the law perfectly with a righteous judgment.

consequence in bringing in original sin. When Adam sinned, he brought in original sin, the first sin, and all the curses that belong to it (*cf.* Romans 5). This was an offense against God's justice, holiness, and majesty. Adam's disobedience merited, earned, a condemnation so great that men can never through their own powers reverse the effects of the fall. The fall brought mankind into an estate of *sin* and *misery.* How is Adam's sin applied to all men? It is applied by credit. Adam's original sin is credited to man's account by God. Adam is cursed, and so all men are cursed in him as if they ate the fruit themselves. All the corruption that goes along with that original sin is spread to *all men.* This is true even from the very conception of a man, Psalm 51:5, "In sin did my mother conceive me." From the time a person is made up of the egg and sperm, the moment they connect into the zygote, the fertilized egg, they are sinners, in a broken covenant, credited with Adam's sin. This original sin has poisoned man's nature. As a result, man's nature is such that it is darkened and depraved so much so that it cannot but sin against God in every way in that state all the time without the possibility of not sinning. "...that every imagination of the thoughts of his heart was only evil continually," (Gen. 6:5). When the zygote is confirmed in God's providence, the person that is made of that union, is fallen, and will as they grow stand in total opposition to God, in fact, be at *war* with him, and will loathe him. People hate the idea that they are called evil by God upon conception, being wicked, and depraved, and fallen, and lost. "I'm a good person," they think. "People are generally good," they think. "I've always loved God in some way," they think. Such talk *shows* their depravity. The Apostle quoting the Psalms sums this up, "There is none that understandeth, there is none that seeketh after God. They are all gone out of the way, they are together become unprofitable; there is none that doeth good, no, not one. Their throat is an open sepulchre; with their tongues they have used deceit; the poison of asps is under their lips: Whose mouth is full of cursing and bitterness: Their feet are swift to shed blood: Destruction and misery are in their ways: And the way of peace have they not known: There is no fear of God before their eyes," (Rom. 3:11-18). Men hate holiness, and they hate to have lives that reflect God's holiness. They have no desire for life-reformation in such a state. Corner a hypocrite in their speech, in their profession, speak about the necessity of holiness, and all their thoughts about religion fall to nothing. They are not holy, nor are they interested in holiness. Religion and holiness are two very different things; for one can be very religious without ever being holy. Zygotes are prone to do evil all their days as they grow into men and women. They sell, "themselves to do evil in the sight of the LORD, to provoke him to anger," (2 Kings 17:17). They drink evil, "How much more abominable and filthy is man, which drinketh iniquity like water?" (Job 15:16). They even commit so much sin, and they transgress God's commandments so constantly, that they weary themselves in it. "... and weary themselves to commit iniquity," (Jer. 9:5). This original sin that presses men to commit all the actual sins they do is in what is called their *depravity,* profaneness, defilement, as Isaiah said; filled with the curse of God. It is universal in all men in all parts of their constitution. There is not a part of a man that is left untouched by that defilement. His mind, emotions, affections, will, and heart are all defiled, they are all profane in God's sight. They, as the prophet preached, "draw iniquity with cords of vanity, and sin as it were with a cart rope," (Isa. 5:18). All such people draw sin in such a way as to market it to others, and think such is acceptable. As if in the market they are pulling this sin-cart to sell their sin to others, and others will come and buy it, partake of it, engage in it. "...they are wise to do evil, but to do good they have no knowledge," (Jer. 4:22). Adam has given them a bad record and a bad heart. The bad record comes from Adam credited to them in the curse that they are conceived in, and the bad heart is the outworking of all they will do in transgression of or lack of conformity to God's law because of it. "The heart is deceitful above all things, and desperately wicked: who can know it?" (Jer. 17:9). People hate to hear, "Your heart is desperately wicked and evil." But this is God's commentary on the state of men in sin, because they broke the everlasting covenant when they sinned in

Adam.[8] All the exercises God would have men do to be holy and happy, they reject and do all that makes men miserable and wicked and they do it like people groping for some purpose in the dark. "We grope for the wall like the blind, and we grope as if we had no eyes: we stumble at noonday as in the night; we are in desolate places as dead men," (Isa. 59:10). *Isaiah* said that in the Old Testament. This wickedness against God is inherent in every soul cursed with the curse of Adam, under the bondage of sin, which they can never escape in their own strength. Original sin is a body of sin made up of many parts. It is a *body* of death. "O wretched man that I am! who shall deliver me from this body of death?" (Rom. 7:24). In that body of death is every sin that could ever be committed and every person is liable to every sin that could ever be committed. People don't think they could ever commit such and such a sin; such is too heinous. They think they are not as bad as *so and so*. Original sin and rebellion and treason against God's covenant argues differently. It is universally affecting them.[9] Throats and lips and tongues and minds and hearts and mouths and feet and heads and every single part, is a *body* of sin.

---

[8] "And God saw that the wickedness of man was great in the earth, and that every imagination of the thoughts of his heart was only evil continually," (Gen. 6:5).

[9] *The 1647 Westminster Larger Catechism* asks in question 27, "What misery did the fall bring upon mankind?" Answer, "The fall brought upon mankind the loss of communion with God, his displeasure and curse; so as we are by nature children of wrath, bond slaves to Satan, and justly liable to all punishments in this world, and that which is to come," (Gen. 3:8, 10, 24; Eph. 2:2-3; 2 Tim. 2:26; Gen. 2:17; Lam. 3:39; Rom. 6:23; Matt. 25:41, 46, Jude 1:7).

They are filled with lust of every kind, traitors to God's law in every way. They are captives to sin, bound in chains of darkness and thrive on evil. They desire to be masters of their own destiny, and a slave to no one but their own desires, copying their father Adam, copying their father the devil,[10] that crafty angelic serpent and dragon.

And what will they say to God when they come to the Christ's judgment throne, the holiness of the Christ meeting them face to face, on this point? They think, now, while they are alive, that they will say, "I was as good as I could be." "I tried to live a good life." "I am not as bad as others are." No, they won't say any of that because the moment they go to judgment, they will know the holiness of God immediately and by personal experience, and *every mouth will be stopped.* You see, in Revelation, all kinds of people go to judgment. "And the kings of the earth, and the great men, and the rich men, and the chief captains, and the mighty men, and every bondman, and every free man," See here the kinds of men listed – those in authority, those rich, those poor, those slaves, those famous, those who lead armies that have a show of power, ... and then? "...hid themselves in the dens and in the rocks of the mountains; and said to the mountains and rocks, Fall on us, and hide us from the face of him that sitteth on the throne, and from the wrath of the Lamb: for the great day of his wrath is come;

---

[10] "Ye are of your father the devil, and the lusts of your father ye will do," (John 8:44).

and who shall be able to stand?" (Rev. 6:15-17). "And they shall go into the holes of the rocks, and into the caves of the earth, for fear of the LORD, and for the glory of his majesty, when he ariseth to shake terribly the earth," (Isa. 2:19). This is an instantaneous revelation of the fall in them without any doubt or question about their *evil* natures. None of them will make any excuses, but will hide, or try to hide, from the wrath of Christ against sin which they know then will be terrible. They will trade Adam's fig leaf to try and cover themselves with rocks and mountains (Rev. 6).

What is the outcome, what is the finality of original sin, and all the actual sins a person commits in this life? When God through Jesus Christ judges all those in original sin that die in their sin, and die unrepentant to God, after that sentence of condemnation is given, which the sinner will in no way contest, then follows everlasting death; is everlasting death bad? The wicked are separated from the blessed presence of God, the glory of God, and the benefits of Jesus Christ in Paradise. Christ comes to restore Paradise, but they are omitted from that fall-reversing restoration. They are punished with eternal turmoil with the most bitter and tormenting thoughts about their life and sins, and they will replay and rethink all their choices for all time, in all their wickedness and sins which will be revealed to them forever. They will have a conscious knowledge of all they gained in this life piled around them to consider it forever as the Apostle James says, which stand as a *witness against them*. They will be punished by God in an everlasting hell. They will be tormented in the spiritual and material furnace of fire. They will have fellowship with their father the devil, and his demonic angels, for they did his works; and be tormented by them and others there, one against another, in a perpetual chaos and downward spiral of eternal misery. Is sin worth any of that, much less the wrath of God forever upon them? No, it is not worth it.

Such people will be in both body and soul tormented with a horror and anguish and punishment which words can barely express, a horror, an exceedingly great anguish as they, through their senses and feelings are made eternally aware of God's holy wrath poured out on them personally to their just amount. "And they shall go forth, and look upon the carcases of the men that have transgressed against me: for their worm shall not die, neither shall their fire be quenched; and they shall be an abhorring unto all flesh," again, Isaiah said that, (Isa. 66:24). Jesus Christ calls such torment: punishment, hell fire, unquenchable fire, the worm that does not die, weeping, gnashing of teeth, outer darkness, damnation, the second death, which is their due because the wages of sin is death.[11] "Fear, and

---

[11] "Hell is the spiritual and material furnace of fire where its damned victims, in their minds, bodies, and souls, are eternally tormented to the full degree and capacity of their beings by God, the devil and his demons, damned human beings, and themselves, through their memories and consciences, without any possibility of relief by mercy nor pity from God." For a full discussion of this topic, see my

the pit, and the snare, are upon thee, O inhabitant of the earth," (Isa. 24:17), this is part of the passage at hand just a few verses later in our text. "Look what Adam's sin did to you," the prophet is crying out, "and look what your sin does before God." The fall of Adam brought in the death of himself, the death of all men, and also, Adam's death brought in the necessity of the death of Christ.

Consider briefly here the death of Christ. Christ is called the second Adam or the last Adam (1 Cor. 15:45). He comes to restore that which was lost; great was its fall but not greater than Christ is a Savior. I remind you what Christ said to one of the thieves on the cross, "And Jesus said unto him, Verily I say unto thee, Today shalt thou be with me in paradise," (Luke 23:43). "To him that overcometh will I give to eat of the tree of life, which is in the midst of the paradise of God." (Rev. 2:7). Paradise was lost, but through Christ, and his work alone, Paradise is restored. He is called in this the last Adam who brings life and happiness through obedience in his life, and obedience in his death. "... the last Adam was made a quickening spirit," (1 Cor. 15:45). God's plan was that the Christ would die on the cross as a satisfaction and substitutionary atonement for the sin of his people, forsaken by the Father as a sin offering for original sin and actual sin. "For he hath made him to be sin for us, who knew no sin; that we might be made the righteousness of God in him," (2 Cor. 5:21).

---

work, *Eternity Weighed in the Balance: The Bible's Teaching on Heaven, Hell and Salvation.*

Christ became the curse. The ground is cursed in the fall, cursed in Isaiah's prophesy with blood, and Christ bleeds on the ground in redemption becoming the curse and taking the defilement and profaneness. Why a crown of thorns? Because even creation is redeemed by the Redeemer and remade anew. "Christ hath redeemed us from the curse of the law, being made a curse for us: for it is written, Cursed is every one that hangeth on a tree," (Gal. 3:13). Isaiah says, in the passage, "Then the moon shall be confounded, and the sun ashamed, when the LORD of hosts shall reign in mount Zion, and in Jerusalem, and before his ancients gloriously," (Isa. 24:23).

This Redeemer rescues sinners who are lost and fallen in Adam. The devil, the crafty serpent and dragon, that angelic deceiver, deceived Eve in the garden, and she gave the forbidden fruit to Adam who was there with her, so Adam ate, and sinners were plunged into misery by that *one* sin. Christ comes to rescue sinners, bruising the head of the serpent, recovering of lapsed sinners, comes incarnate as God, to take on human flesh, as the first proclamation of the Gospel is set in the context of the fall of man in Genesis 3:15. He is the one which is promised to crush the serpent's head, and consequently to rescue sinners from the serpent, and is described as, "the Seed of the woman," taking upon flesh to be Immanuel, "God with us," (Matthew 1:23). He comes with a Kingly authority to work his power to reverse the fall in men, to deliver them from the kingdom of darkness into the Kingdom of God.

The Christ restores Paradise ... *better.* Christ restores what Adam lost, and more. In Rev. 2:7 it is Jesus who gives the fruit of paradise to the saints and those victorious in the Spirit. "To him that overcometh will I give to eat of the tree of life, which is in the midst of the paradise of God," (Rev. 2:7). Jesus restores paradise by his work and merit. In teaching his disciples, John the Baptist sent them to the Christ to ask, "Are you the one or should we look for another?" How did Jesus answer? "What did the *prophet Isaiah say,* "Then the eyes of the blind shall be opened, and the ears of the deaf shall be unstopped. Then shall the lame man leap as an hart, and the tongue of the dumb sing: for in the wilderness shall waters break out, and streams in the desert," (Isa. 35:5). Christ affirms the prophet's *Gospel* of the good tidings of God's holy work in the Mediator. And what must they do in order to be rescued from the fall? Shall we look for another. No, no, just look to the Christ. Looking, believing, exercising faith in the One God sends.

One must have saving faith in this Christ to be rescued from the curse of Adam. "Faith brings believers from Paradise, through Paradise, to Paradise."[12] It brings them from paradise fallen, to paradise restored, to paradise fulfilled. In order to navigate that road, one must believe in the Christ as Savior and Deliverer from

---

[12] Roberts, Francis, *Mysterium and Medulla Bibliorum, the Mystery and Marrow of the Bible,* (London: R.W., 1657) 133.

the curse, that he is the only one that can rescue men from sin, death and hell, rescue men from God's wrath. That one must set belief and faith on those truths, that Gospel content. This is not a *blind* faith, but a faith resting on Christ; not in mere words, not in an ungrounded hope of, "something *might* be done." Faith rests in the person of Jesus Christ, and it believes the word of God, and the Spirit makes those truths weighty and heavy in the soul, for there is no condemnation to those who are in Christ Jesus, for now the law is fulfilled in him. The Lord Jesus, the great Shepherd and Bishop of souls, that Lamb of God who *taketh away the sins of the world,* who promised paradise to the repenting thief, pardons and forgives all sins known and unknown, for all sinners who come to him for rest, and they can and may be redeemed by Christ the Savior. In him alone is restoration, and rescue from original sin, (this we will speak more about in the fourth principle).

Consider that sin in sinners is a most important principle. You came into the world under the curse of Adam, and in original sin, with all your actual sins now attached to it. Original sin is more than simply feeling guilty over your sin, it is a defilement, a profaneness of your soul in the light of God's majesty and holiness; it is an objective reality that has subjective feelings attached to it. It is that God counts lost sinners as defiling his creation, because you have transgressed his laws, you have changed the ordinances of God, you have broken the ancient covenant of works in Adam, right along side of Adam *as if you ate the fruit yourself.* In this, sin continually assaults you day in and day out; it looks to master you. It is continually pulling you down and away from God. This sin in you is like a pulse that presses you moment by moment to have vain thoughts, corrupt imaginations, wicked desires, and run to new heights of it all in idolatrous living. You might say, "I'm not an idolater." Sin is idolatry against God. "...fornication, uncleanness, inordinate affection, evil concupiscence, and covetousness, which is idolatry," (Col. 3:5); for your mind is a factory of idols. All you do as a sinner in an unconverted state is produce vain ideas and desires that feed your own pride and covetousness in everything because it is love of self over love of God. When you love yourself and do for yourself more than for God, it is a blinding work that you do. You love yourself and you hate God. You love yourself and you hate Christ. You might think, "well, I've never said I hate Christ." But, Christ said, "He that is not with me is against me; and he that gathereth not with me scattereth abroad," (Matt. 12:30). Unless you are *sold out* for Jesus Christ, you are not for him, and he counts you a God-hater. Those unconverted by Christ's eminent means of grace are not sold out for Christ, they are God-haters. Christ draws that line in the sand, and you must argue with him if you don't like what he said. Self-love blinds you where you are unable to see any sin that you do, really, unless it is a sin that is culturally unacceptable, or makes you feel bad. A person will stop beating their children and wife because they don't want to get into trouble with the law. They stop robbing banks because they don't want to go to jail. These sinners, like you if you are unconverted, don't do anything for God's glory, not even when they help a little old lady across the street because they do it for the wrong reasons; they don't do it for God's glory nor in holiness. But you that are still in your sins, you don't see yourself doing anything so evil, so terrible. You pass life off as being pretty good as a person, because you think, "no one is perfect." You believe that everything you do, you do as you would like them to be, and so you do whatever you want, or desire. Self-love deceives you into thinking that you are looking out for number one in a good way, and that God will give you a pass, because he grades on a curve (because that is the way you like to think about it) and you are not so bad, not as bad as other people that you know; for *no one is perfect.* But you are missing the point in this, for hell is reserved *for imperfect people.* You are required to be *perfect.* "Thou shalt be perfect with the LORD thy God," (Deut. 18:13). "Be ye therefore perfect, even as your Father which is in heaven is perfect," (Matt. 5:48). You misrepresent original sin and in doing so, miss the importance of the Savior who came to save men from that evil.

To misrepresent original sin is to fail in understanding how one is saved from it. You must see original sin for what it is, the root of all evil that resides in your heart and in all your actions. Do you see yourself as a vile sinner? Job called himself a *worm.* Abraham said he was merely *dust and ashes*. Peter coward from Christ in the boat and said, "depart from me Lord for I am a sinful man." Do you see yourself as the most wicked sinner in the world? If you say "No, I'm not so low, so debase," you may be *still* in your sins. If you deny you are such a worm, dust and ashes, and so low, you are *still* in your sins; "they don't see," Jesus said, "therefore their sin remains." It may be that you claim you haven't really thought about it in such a way, so it doesn't apply to you. This is an *impossibility* for those redeemed by Christ. The redeemed *know* Jesus saves *sinners, i.e.* mourners, poor in spirit, contrite ones, *etc.* He did not come for, "the righteous, but sinners," to call them to repentance.

Or is it that you see yourself with a better nature than most people have? You think, "well, I have this sin reckoned to my account, God hates me and my sin in Adam, and I'm dead in my sins. But how dead am I, really? I know that sin affects me, I'm completely affected in my mind, emotions, and will by the fall. But I also know that I'm not as bad as I can be. I am not as bad as a serial killer. I'm not as bad as a school shooter. I'm not as bad as an evil dictator. Maybe that argues a little bit for my goodness, because I'm not as bad as I could be and certainly not as bad as most people?" No, no, the enmity that is between you and God is infinite because of God's holy character, and it is only reconcilable through Jesus Christ. You are a child of *wrath*, and God's displeasure remains on you, being dead in sin, spiritually still born in God's eyes, by original sin. The result of the credit of Adam's sin to you is a "deadness" in sin; it is not simply a hinderance, it is the origin of all your evil; and redeemed sinners never think of themselves in the way of "I'm not so bad." Redeemed sinners see themselves as disgusting a thing, with nothing in them that is deserving of any praise, giving all glory and honor to Jesus Christ. It means you cannot possibly please God unless God redeems you and changes your reckoning status in his sight from under Adam to under the Christ, the second Adam. Even if you argue that you are not as bad as you could be, you are still imperfect. One sin is being imperfect. God says, "Whosoever hath sinned against me, him will I blot out of my book," (Exod. 32:33). So there you have it: to be imperfect, with only one sin, would be an unacceptable state if *perfection* is God's prerequisite in his covenant. It means that though you are not as bad as you could be in your outward actions, you are still under condemnation because you are not perfect, and you have not upheld the law of God as God requires; and like Adam, you have transgressed the covenant. You need Christ; you still need supernatural repentance, you still need to believe in God's way of holiness; so *look to him, and be ye saved.*

What about sin in the redeemed saint? You know that original sin hinders everything. Original sin is an infection of our nature which remains in the redeemed saint in this life even after being born again. It holds certain wayward consequences as a result. You as redeemed are angrier with yourself for your corruptions that still remain in you. Little offenses, all sin as sin, you hate. When God's glory is tainted by your sin by way of perspective, the reflex is to repent and gain a clean conscience before God, seek pardon and forgiveness as quickly as possible. You have big sins, little sins, secret faults, and besetting sins. The life of a redeemed believer in this fallen world is a hard one, and God calls mourners blessed, and poor in spirit those he will look at, those seeing their need of him. Jesus doesn't say your life is going to be a bed of roses or a walk in the park. He says that you must pick up your cross and follow him. The Christian life is about crosses; that's because this world is riddled with sin.

You are as a redeemed believer stern and critical against all your sin. You can't tolerate sin for any length of time, even upon its first rising in your soul. There is a great combat that ensues in this; the flesh is warring against the Spirit. For even when you sin, you don't sin like an unregenerate person sins. The original corruption in them is bondage, but to you it is part of God's sanctifying work in you. You live as a sin-hater, and that's very hard. Your love of God causes you to have a hatred of sin and the fall, and are motioned by the Spirit to hate it further day by day. You avoid it not only in adversity, but also in prosperity when everything is calm and quiet in your life. You, like Joseph (Genesis 39:9), see sin as sin and do not flee from one sin, but you flee from *all* sin, as sin, just as God hates all sin; you *strive* for that. Sin ought never to be your habitual and ordinary practice. You do not run headlong into sin as a *way of living*. You know that God's grace working in you through Christ is inconsistent with a wicked life. You know that you must have more than a mere profession, but a life answerable to your profession; and yes, that is hard. But you live that life willingly, for you desire to have no part of defiling yourself before God and desire to honor the Christ who has covered you with his blood, and his everlasting covenant of grace. God's love to you has so moved your conscience, and given you tools for sanctification that you happily employ them. What a gracious thing it is to stand firm in Christ and his work, and walk in the Spirit, being victorious as a soldier before the great King!

As a redeemed believer, you are very sensible of your original sin, even your heart sins, or your besetting sins. You know that sin looks to master you, but you will not have it. You know you fall into it, and are disgusted by it, and Christ is there to lift you up and pardon you at every turn, even seventy times seven; you are very happy for that. Yet, you strive to break off from sin, and kill it by the Spirit; push it back into the grave, into the casket where the old man is decaying; it comes after you again, it's relentless, but you press into the kingdom; you are a violent solider for Christ. You think to yourself, "sin is what plunged humanity in the abyss. And these sins all come out of that original sin that dwells in me. It brings forth innumerable other sins, and what will I do to kill it? This sin was the power, and strength, and head of other sins, and shall I not fight against it? This sin was Satan's castle of defense. Shall it not be battered down, and not one stone left on another? How shall I do this but by the Deliverer, the Christ, and his blood, which covers all my sins, and empowers me for service." The wicked, they entertain sin and love it and follow it, and it leads them as a servant in bondage to it. But not you. You will not allow sin to ruin your worship of the Father. Sin *ruins* worship. You will not allow sin to ruin relationships with others. Sin *ruins* relationships. You will not allow sin to ruin holy duties before the Great King. Sin mixes with our duties *all the time.* The best works you have, as a godly Christian, have sin clinging in them. You know that only Christ's blood makes atonement. Bring Christ to every duty, and God will cover it in his blood. How I wish we would all do that with everything! You will not allow sin to ruin your belief in pressing you towards unbelief. Sin mixes in you with grace and pushes you towards unbelief; that's where the devil wants you to go, in the way of the unbeliever. He desires you to do what Adam did in heeding lies in the garden. "Did God really say?" To give into it makes you to be atheistical in practice. "Do I really need to do what Christ said?" As a matter of fact, yes, you do. "And why call ye me, Lord, Lord, and do not the things which I say?" (Luke 6:46). Jesus was the one who asked this! So no, you will not take the path of an unbeliever, you will not walk or stand or sit in the sinner's way (Psalm 1). You know sin is active in you, and that you must oppress it rather than it oppressing you. Sin is an active principle in you as it remains until the day of glory when you go to heaven. You know it's there, and that it will not leave in this life without a fight. Your old man is dead, but the remaining sin is still there trying to revive the old man, to no use, because Christ has broken those shackles for you. Christ will have his victory over it in you if you trust and follow him. Sin is not cured (taken away in its entirety) in this life, and you know that too, but that is not an excuse in you, as it is with some. Sin still remains, to make you long after heaven. It still remains, to make you look to Christ for help. It still remains, to make you vigilant against evil. It still remains as a means to press you to strive for holiness as it rages against you to buffet you, that you will seek *Christ's* holy grace which is sufficient. You have been released from sins bondage and slavery by his blood, it now no longer reigns in you. And yet, you know that all men have sinned in Adam and are under the curse of God, but Christ frees you from this curse, being made a curse for you. This we will study further in the fourth principle of these good tidings of the Gospel, that Christ the Redeemer, Christ alone, saves men from the curse.

Principle 4:
The Giving of the Christ and His Garment of Salvation

"For I the LORD love judgment, I hate robbery for burnt offering; and I will direct their work in truth, and I will make an everlasting covenant with them. And their seed shall be known among the Gentiles, and their offspring among the people: all that see them shall acknowledge them, that they are the seed which the LORD hath blessed. I will greatly rejoice in the LORD, my soul shall be joyful in my God; for he hath clothed me with the garments of salvation, he hath covered me with the robe of righteousness, as a bridegroom decketh himself with ornaments, and as a bride adorneth herself with her jewels. For as the earth bringeth forth her bud, and as the garden causeth the things that are sown in it to spring forth; so the Lord GOD will cause righteousness and praise to spring forth before all the nations," (Isaiah 61:8-11).

In this prophecy there is the good news of deliverance in the Christ, who is the only Savior, the Healer and Deliverer. Isaiah's message is one of *proclamation*, on behalf of God; since all ministers are to speak, not what they want, but what God gives through being sensitive to his leading and Spirit as they consult the word of God. God's message is given to the *watchman* by the Spirit who anoints him to preach and proclaim. His message is for the poor, the imprisoned, the broken, and all those who mourn (verse 1). He comes as a herald, anointed of God, to proclaim salvation, godliness and judgment (verse 2). This message is a comfort to those who mourn. His message is beauty, anointing, praise and righteousness, in which they will be made free, comforted, and supported. His preached message replaced ashes, mourning, and a spirit of heaviness (maybe even translated as *colorlessness,* or *dullness*). His preaching turns the heaviness of sin into that which is beautiful in the Savior. If Jerusalem, the church, is going to be restored, (verse 4), that it would be raised up and repaired, it needs a new spirit to be beautiful.

In the second section, verses 4-7, there is a repetition of 58:12, and the theme of restoration of God's people is given (*cf.* 49:8, 60:10). Here is found a construction of buildings, the work of the lands, gardens, fields and vineyards. The work of the temple brought into scope, where the people are then called priests, and their testimony from other people outside of themselves, will regard them as ministers. God has given salvation and has restored the church in seeing all this occur.

Then God speaks, "I the Lord ..." (verses 8-9). He will establish, set and secure the covenant with his people. God is committed to the covenant, will not let it wallow or wobble, will uphold it, but the people must follow him in it. All injustice must be cast away, and God desires through this kingdom of priests, to not only bless the church, but also bless those outside the church with an eye to bring them inside the church, (verse 9). This Spirit-anointed preacher of good news to the poor and oppressed is one who previously, in 50:4–9 and 52:13–53:12, suffers for his people to provide them with the means of drawing near to God in reversing the fall. This anointed One, is God's Mediator to the needy and those distressed as a result of not merely physical oppression, but sin and the curse of the fall. Christ identified himself directly with this role in Luke 4:14–21. When he read this passage, he only read the first verse and part of verse 2 and stopped. The *now and not yet* character of the passage shows what Christ will do, and still there is more to come. And yet, there must be a response to the coming of the Messiah. He came first as a sin offering, to proclaim freedom. He will come again to establish the fully rebuilt Kingdom of God in the final consummation of all things; such a Kingdom is at hand but only in him. There is a *taste* of that *now*, but a fullness of that in the *not yet.* (The tenet of "now and not yet" is a constant biblical theme running through time until the end of all things.)

Then verse 10, "I will greatly rejoice in the LORD, my soul shall be joyful in my God; for he hath clothed me with the garments of salvation, he hath covered me with the robe of righteousness, as a bridegroom decketh himself with ornaments, and as a bride adorneth herself with her jewels," (Isa. 61:10). *I will greatly rejoice in the LORD.* Why is there a cause of rejoicing in all this? God will not leave his church destitute and naked. He will beautify and adorn it with his gifts and graces. This Isaiah feels and labors to express. What rejoicing is he expressing? "My soul shall be joyful in my God, for he hath clothed me with the garments of salvation, he has covered me with the robe of righteousness." Garments of Salvation These clothes, these garments, are of salvation. ישׁע (yesha`) or ישׁע (yay'-shah) deliverance or salvation, through *Yeshua,* or *Joshua,* as then translated in the New Testament as *Iaysoos,* or as we have it *Savior.* These are beautiful garments of salvation which is a cause of rejoicing brought by *Iaysoos,* the Savior. This is because Isaiah is testifying of the robe of righteousness that God gives his people as a garment of salvation through the Christ. And in this is assumed, that when God pardons sin, he grants righteousness. If sins are pardoned, if a sinner is pardoned, by God, he is made legally righteous by this covering; for to be *pardoned* is only half the job, and he must be then covered. This righteousness is imputed, given like a cloak or garment that covers them. This is an announcement or declaration that the sinner is covered by the righteousness of the Herald, the Healer, the One on whom God has anointed to preach glad tidings to the poor, to come and cover their nakedness. What kind of standing is this where one can rejoice in the covering of a reckoned righteousness to their account? It is, no doubt, perfect, superlative, and most excellent coming from this Savior and Deliverer.

In essence, Isaiah has been *Jesused* in this, being saved by the righteous garments of the Savior's work and merit. This giving of a garment by God, this giving of Christ and his righteousness, contains all that Isaiah has said not only in this chapter, but also in previous ones that relate to this Messiah. The Savior's work and merit in his mediation, his call to the offices of prophet, priest and king, his special work of declaring God, his sending in covenant by the Father, his ability to bind up the broken-hearted, to proclaim liberty to the captives and such things; Isaiah has seen *all of this.* Here God is accepting of sinners who are clothed with the garment of the Messiah's righteousness and rejoice in his salvation. In turn, Isaiah rejoices in this, because God has clothed and covered him with the garments of salvation, and with the robe of his righteousness. What could Isaiah possibly mean by these words, but the pure, spotless robe of Christ's righteousness given to poor sinners that they are covered in the sight of God from all their sin and wickedness? What would cause the prophet to rejoice *more* than this? God makes his people beautiful, and covers all their sins and deformities, and makes them appear as beautiful and lovely in the eyes of God, as a bride does, who is adorned with unmatched beauty. Verse 10, "As a bridegroom decketh himself with ornaments." He is decked with ornaments, which literally, is a headdress, of the capping ornaments of his attire. The *superlative* excellencies of the Savior are found here, for their Maker is their Husband. "And as a bride adorneth herself with jewels." This is the affect of Isaiah's marriage and union to God the Savior. It is as a bride is covered, decorated, by the salvation of *Yeshua*. As a bride readied for her husband, righteousness and salvation, given as garments, adorns the bride and further ornaments her with jewels; all the gifts and graces that make a bride a bride, or a church a church under the salvation of the Savior. The bride has a joy in her justification before God. Isaiah 61:10 says again, "I will greatly rejoice in the Lord, my soul shall be joyful in my God; for he hath clothed me with the garments of salvation, he hath covered me with the robes of righteousness." The metaphor occurs also in Psalm 71:6 and 109:18. God clothes his church with "righteousness" derived from himself (Isaiah 54:17), and they are saved as a result. The church is made the bride, and united through the work of the Savior, to him as a bridegroom who, "decketh himself with a priestly crown, and as a bride who adorneth herself with her jewels." The doctrine could be stated in this way: that righteousness and salvation should be the substance of the church's rejoicing and thanksgiving (verses 10-11).

Consider again the previous principles so far. 1) God exists. 2) He has made man in his image (knowledge, righteousness and holiness with dominion). 3) Man fell from paradise breaking the everlasting covenant of works. And now, the fourth principle of the good news is: God has not left all sinners to perish under Adam's curse, but has given those redeemed the righteousness of Christ as a garment to cover them by the Covenant of Grace.

All the superlative excellencies and perfections which are in Christ's person, which make him the very righteousness of God, are given to sinners on their conversion; they enter a new covenant with God (God does all he does by way of covenant).[1] God has one Savior that remedies the fall of Adam, and rescues repentant sinners from death, hell and God's eternal wrath for sin. What Christ accomplishes in his saving work is not indiscriminately given to all for possession, but indiscriminately preached to all men that they might possess it in order to be saved. God has a Savior, and in that Savior alone, in *Yeshua* Messiah, men can be forgiven and converted. If they are, they are covered. If they are covered, they rejoice. If they rejoice, they honor the Savior with thanksgiving.

Forgiveness of sin is forgiveness of *all* sin. The garment or robe of Christ's righteousness, of his salvation, is so large that it covers the least sin, to the greatest sin; but, it covers *all* of a sinner's sin. Some men think that they are more of a sinner than Christ is a

---

[1] *1647 Westminster Confession of Faith*, 7:1, "The distance between God and the creature is so great that although reasonable creatures do owe obedience unto him as their Creator, yet they could never have any fruition of him as their blessedness and reward but by some voluntary condescension on God's part, which he hath been pleased to express by way of covenant."

Savior, but this is impossible. Christ, being God, when he forgives, forgives all sin, not some sin.[2] What a terrible thought that is, to repent, to come to Christ, to believe he is the Savior and find out that only *some* sins would be forgiven, where a person's work must be done to eradicate the rest of sin by one's own power? Is that not the doctrine of Popish Antichrist, and the Arminian heretic? More work must be done for them in their theological views. How depressing to place the end of salvation into the hands of sinners!

Jesus Christ does away with all sins in a penitent sinner, all past sins, all present sins and all future sins, if they are converted by his Spirit and born again. This robe of his righteous that he imparts is all encompassing and all covering. There is no little sin that slips by. There is no small sin that it misses. There is no large sin that doesn't fit under its covering. There are no holes in his garment of salvation. Once they have this robe of righteousness on, it covers them completely. This is the simplicity of Isaiah's Gospel message, his good tidings. Men are to believe God in the simplicity of which he speaks. What does he say in these verses of Isaiah? "...opening of the prison to them that are bound"

---

[2] "All manner of sin and blasphemy shall be forgiven unto men," (Matt. 12:31). And, "Thou hast forgiven the iniquity of thy people, thou hast covered all their sin." (Psa. 85:2). As the prophet says, "...the people that dwell therein shall be forgiven their iniquity." (Isa. 33:24). And, "Come now, and let us reason together, saith the LORD: though your sins be as scarlet, they shall be as white as snow; though they be red like crimson, they shall be as wool," (Isa. 1:18).

"...clothing them with the garments of salvation," "...covering them with the robe of righteousness." This God does for those penitent sinners that look to God for salvation, that look to the Messiah for his saving grace. He will be merciful if men come in a way, the only way, of salvation and righteousness, to gain from God through the Christ, to have an interest in him, this spiritual garment he freely bestows and holds out to them.

In the *theoretical* realm of considering this, once eternal mercy is bestowed and given, the pardon and salvation itself is unchanging, just like the promise God makes to save men, which is unchanging; for his word is settled in heaven (Psalm 119:89-94). If a man believes in the good tidings, and receives this robe, he gains it *one* time; once is enough to do the job; he does not go out and buy it again and again by some price or some fleshly means. It is freely bestowed once, and when it is given, it is given *forever* to them. They cannot lose it. Sins are no more when Christ pardons and forgives. When men come to Christ, he takes all their burdens away from them at the foot of the cross, and they tumble down off their shoulders and roll into his empty tomb. God reckons, *declares*, a sinner's account clean, without any condemnation or vengeance against them if they are converted and justified.[3] No one will be able to lay any further charges to the sinner's name, even if they are

---

[3] God no longer punishes them in their sin, for he punished Christ for them.

accused by the great adversary to God's very face. As the serpentine adversary (that old dragon the devil) did with Joshua the high priest, who received from Christ new clothes, his old ones were done away with (Zech. 3:3ff). Such a one is covered, given a robe of righteousness, in which God is wholly satisfied. Celebrities and famous people, rich people, are clothed with very costly clothes and very rich attire. The sinner's garments are unlike those, for penitent sinners are clothed with the white pure robes of Christ's righteousness that can never fade nor wear out, where there is no need of any other robe, or any other covering. Let those others have their fancy clothes and expensive attire bought again and again. John Favel said, "Let those that have full tables, heavy purses, rich lands, but no Christ, be rather objects of your pity than envy."[4]

This salvation is fitly called, the *Garment of Salvation*, given in the covenant of Christ's grace. The Covenant of Grace is the answer to the Covenant of Works. Christ's work outworks Adam's disobedience by an infinitude of power and glory. What Adam lost Christ restores. Paradise lost in Adam is paradise restored in Christ. What sinners have been cast into, Christ can redeem them out of. The head of the serpent is *crushed* in his work; it is a fatal blow. And in such a covenant, he gives sinners *grace*, spiritual benefits they

---

[4] Flavel, John, *The Works of John Flavel*, Volume 2, (Carlisle, PA: Banner of Truth Trust: 1995) 212.

do not deserve, freely, and clothes them with garments that are in fact *called* salvation.

The Bible has a great amount to say about clothing. It is especially full of this idea of a robe of righteousness that causes sinners to rejoice. "All thy garments smell of myrrh, and aloes, and cassia, out of the ivory palaces, whereby they have made thee glad." (Psa. 45:8); they *smell* of the covenant. "I put on righteousness," (Job 29:14). "Bring forth the best robe, and put it on him," (Luke 15:22). There are many Scriptures of this sort. What can be said about them? Garments are made to cover the nakedness of the fall, which is a covering over the infinite shame of sin against God. Such a saving garment hides their nakedness, hides their shame, hides what they have as a result of the fall. Clothes were naturally bestowed on men, but prepared for men *because* of the fall. They are generally tailored to fit people in particular and must be the right size and shape for each particular person. Why do clothes exist? It is because *sin* exists, and yet people are so fascinated by clothing; there are whole industries dedicated to clothing; people strut around with special, new clothing in which they pay a great amount of money for. Yet at the fall, God clothed Adam and Eve with the skins of animals to *cover* them. They needed a covering, they needed to *hide their nakedness*. Clothing, now, has turned *cute*. Clothing as a type, though, covers the fall; and it should remind people *of the fall*.

Various kinds of clothes tell people who see them who they are or where they are from. What pictures come to mind when these terms are used: a king, a knight, a surgeon, a policeman, a Scotsman, an English Guard, a marine; you see the mere *mentioning* of the name sets a picture in the mind of what that garment would look like. In the military, various ranks have various markings on their clothes to distinguish their very ranks. Clothes are *very* distinguishing things in their nature.

Clothes are often used for protection. Protective clothes help protect people from the weather, or the jungle or the forest, or the sea, and various kinds of clothes are worn as protection in such environments. An expedition to Mt. Everest, a deep-sea dive, a cowboy's ranch, all have certain kinds of protective clothing fit for those places. Warm clothes keep people warm, like those who live in Alaska, or in the deep mountainous regions of Tibet, who deal with inordinate amounts of snow. If they did not have warm clothing, they would die in those places.

Clothes biblically even distinguish between men and women, although the current wickedness of the planet and its political correctness and identity culture is continually trying to overthrow that. "The woman shall not wear that which pertaineth unto a man, neither shall a man put on a woman's garment: for all that do so are abomination unto the LORD thy God," (Deut. 22:5); *men and women* are to be righteously reflected by their clothing. Nations and countries even have clothing that can many times distinguish one person from another by country. Someone from India and someone from China have particular clothes; one can look at a person and see the difference. Some clothing is religious, like a Genevan robe, or a black suit and black dress for a funeral, or even sackcloth used in mourning (Genesis 37:34).

But the best garment, is the garment that brings eternal joy. It is the garment of all prodigal sinners who come back to the Father, "bring forth the best robe, and put it on him," (Luke 15:22). They have the best robe, there is found the garment of salvation; a gift from the Father, through the Christ by the application of the Holy Spirit. The best robe is Christ's robe of righteousness. It is *very* distinguishing.

Christ's robe of righteousness for sinners is as a garment, very distinguishing indeed. Whoever is like Adam and Eve, whoever is fallen, must necessarily be clothed with a special clothing to cover infinite guilt and sin or they remain lost. God covered them originally in their spiritual deformity and physical nakedness because of sin in Genesis 3:21. The Lord Jesus Christ is the robe of righteousness for the soul, whether that be for the first man Adam, or the last converted soul before the Lord returns. Whoever is *not* covered by him, God still sees his *spiritual deformity.*

In man's fallen nature, he is naturally unrighteous, and has no righteousness in him at all. Such people are vessels of wrath, dead in sin, and fallen. In no natural way do they have any adequate righteousness that God would be satisfied with. What they need must be tailored by the Christ, and bestowed by the Spirit. "And that ye put on the new man, which after God is created in righteousness and true holiness," (Eph. 4:24). What is this? "...put on Christ," (Gal. 3:27). "...greatly rejoice in the LORD," (Isa. 61:10). "...be joyful in my God," (Isa. 61:10). "...he hath clothed me with the garments of salvation, he hath covered me with the robe of righteousness," (Isa. 61:10). This garment of Christ holds in it all grace, all divine virtue, all the spiritual qualifications of the children of God in the sight of God for their eternal good. When someone buys a new set of clothes, if they are of any value, or, as we say here in the mountains of Tennessee, if they will "last in the woods," are very *costly*. Cheap clothes rip and tear quite quickly. This spiritual garment of Christ is very costly, it cost God the life of his dear Son to die on a cross; it cost him his blood-sweat in the garden, his blood poured out on the cross, and his very life. It cost him to be forsaken of the Father. But for sinners to obtain it or purchase it, they have no need of money. This robe of righteousness can be gained without money and without price for them for Christ has already secured the debt owed, as Isaiah says, "ye shall be redeemed without money," (Isa. 52:3). "Ho, every one that thirsteth, come ye to the waters, and he that hath no money; come ye, buy, and eat; yea, come, buy wine and milk without money and without price," (Isa. 55:1). It is a garment of the Spirit that can never wear out, and the longer it's worn the more excellent its virtue is known by the bearer. It cannot become better, but it can be known better. It is never to be taken off, and it cannot be traded or given to another. In fact, it is so special that such a robe of righteousness turns into the very armor of God to be worn in battle; it is a very special garment indeed in this way.

In order to put on Christ, in order to rejoice in salvation, in order to put on the robe of Christ's righteousness, one must look to Christ, repent, believe and have taken off him the clothes of sin; one cannot wear two sets of clothes. "Repent ye therefore, and be converted, that your sins may be blotted out," (Acts 3:19). You see there, supernatural repentance, conversion (change) and then pardon ensues. Before anyone can put on the Lord Jesus Christ, and be clothed with his garment of righteousness, he must have his sins put off. Sin is likened to a garment as well. It is not likened to fine clothes, but *filthy* clothes. It is seen as "filthy rags," (Isa. 64:6), and, "filthy garments," (Zech. 3:3). Sinners must have such things, "taken away," (Zech. 3:4) that he may be clothed with the Spirit and the righteousness of God's Christ. Paul said, "...put off the old man with his deeds," (Col. 3:9). "...And have put on the new man, which is renewed in knowledge after the image of him that created him," (Col. 3:10). This garment of salvation is a *very* protective garment for poor sinners. In it they are protected against the worst supernatural force creation has even known, which is the wrath of God; it is a most terrible plight of infinite intensity. God cursed men in Genesis 3, and God must be appeased and satisfied in his holiness (cf. Romans chapters 1-4). This robe will do that; it is a grand protective covering in this way. They are even defended from the constant accusing nature of their conscience that desires to censure them always before God by wearing this garment. They are defended from the fiery darts of the evil one, from the blows of the devil and his wicked works against them by wearing this garment. It keeps the soul fervent in spirit and zealous in all their duties by wearing this garment. Any heat, fervent prayers, zeal, holiness, burning fires in the soul, are all attributed to Christ's robe of righteousness that covers them, a very special garment indeed in this! For they are told by the King, "...for without me *ye can do nothing*," (John 15:5), in this way they wear his very righteousness as a garment of salvation.

Christ's spiritual garment is *distinguishing*. This robe of righteousness, clearly delineates the saved from the lost. It makes a perfect distinction between these two kinds of people. If a person has this robe, they are saved and on their way to heaven, accepted in God's sight. If a person does not have this robe, they are on their way to hell, and accursed in God's sight. This is because Christ's work, his holy garment of salvation, distinguishes believers from unbelievers, the godly from the wicked, the sheep from the goats. "If so be that being clothed we shall not be found naked," (2 Cor. 5:3). One is either naked before God's sight, or one is clothed with the robe of righteousness that covers their nakedness. There are only two kinds of people: clothed and unclothed in this way.

Not only does this garment spiritually make a difference between people, saved and lost, but it outwardly demonstrates this to others. When people put on Christ, when they believe by faith in the Savior, when they are changed by the Spirit of God and given this robe of righteousness, having repented of their sins, and come to God solely on the merits of his dear Son, they will then *demonstrate the purity of this robe.* They will be known by their robe, their holy life, by this white garment of salvation that causes them to do two things in this text: both rejoice and be thankful.

This is why Isaiah could rejoice in God, rejoice in Yesha, *Yeshua,* salvation. He was clothed with the robe of righteousness, having on the beautiful garments of Jesus Christ, the garments of salvation. He was *Jesused,* or rather, saved, redeemed, covered, *and clothed.*

The garment of Christ's work is exceedingly glorious, and beatifies its wearer. The remedy provided in Jesus Christ for the elect by the covenant of grace is based on the robe of his pure righteousness. Hosea 13:9, "O Israel, thou hast destroyed thyself; but in me is thine help." God, for the glory of his rich covenant of grace, has revealed salvation in his word to save sinners, by faith in Jesus Christ, the eternal Son of God. This is by virtue of and according to the tenor of the covenant, made and agreed on, between God the Father and God the Son, in the counsel of the Trinity, before the world began. And such is based on Christ's righteousness to atone for his people and clothe them with a robe whiter than the light.

God freely chose to life, a certain number of lost mankind, for the glory of his rich grace, and gave, before the world began, to the Son (Matt. 25:34; John 17:1ff; Eph. 1:4; Heb. 4:3; Rev. 13:8). This Son is the one and only appointed Redeemer, who is *white and ruddy*, as the *beloved* (Song of Solomon 5:10). Who is (white) divine that took on himself that body (ruddy) that the Father prepared,[5] to offer up a sacrifice pleasing to God – the God man, *white and ruddy* as the church's description of the beloved in the Song of Songs, who is divine and human. He submitted himself to the law as a surety for his people, and satisfied the Father's justice for them, by giving obedience in their name, even to the suffering of the cursed death of the cross. He ransomed them from sin and death, and purchased to them his own righteousness and eternal life; with all the benefits of his death. All saving graces leading to eternal life, is by means of his own appointment, applied in due time to every one of them. God received this condition of the Christ being a substitute, before the world began, and in the fulness of time came into the world, was born of the

---

[5] All this speaks to the incarnation, which is replete throughout the Old Testament.

Virgin Mary, subjected himself to the law, and completely paid the ransom on the cross, died, and rose from the death. To accomplish this, Christ was clothed with the offices of *prophet, priest and king*, a prophet to reveal the Father, and to persuade them to believe and obey his word; a priest to offer up an infinite sacrifice, and to intercede for them; and a king, to subdue them to himself and rule them by his appointed ordinances, and to defend them from all their enemies. What kind of a garment is this to discern all such thoughts in it?

In this garment which Christ clothes his people, is that perfect righteousness of every true Christian, which must be more than the righteousness of the scribes and Pharisees. The scribes and Pharisees took great pains to accomplish certain duties of the law, yet they came short because they were infected, and contaminated, by the depravity of the fall; they had no covering and tried to work salvation by human means. They studied the outward part of the duty, but neglected the inward and spiritual part. They went about to establish their own righteousness, and rejected the righteousness of God by faith in the Christ. But a true Christian must have more than all this; he must acknowledge the full extent of the spiritual meaning of the law, and have a respect to all the commandments, and labor to cleanse himself from all filthiness of flesh and spirit, and not lay weight on what service he has done, or shall do to be justified in God's sight, but clothe himself only with the credited and imputed righteousness of Christ, which is the only thing that can hide his nakedness from the holy gaze of the Father; otherwise, he cannot be saved.

Here these good tidings ring so loudly, that its joyful sound might be heard by those that take hold of Christ by faith. That they have heartily embraced the gracious offer of Christ. They by receiving him become the sons of God, and are incorporated into his mystical body, that he may dwell in them, as his temple, and they dwell in him, as in the residence of righteousness and eternal life. There must be in this a contentedness with his sufficiency and this peculiar garment. There is no other place to go, to seek righteousness, or eternal life but by the garment of salvation; there is no other garment. There must be an interest in him alone, in employing and making use of him, in contentment in him, and adhering to him, so that nothing of the world the flesh or the devil may be able to drive their spirits from a knowledge of such a glorious covering.

God gave the Christ that you might live, where the excellencies of the Lord Jesus Christ abound. He is Life (John 1:4), Bread (John 6:48), hidden Manna (Rev. 2:17), Drink (John 6:55), he is all in all (Col. 3:11), and provides all things for believers; even your clothing (Rev. 3:5). The excellencies of Christ, which he communicates to believers, are considered in two main ways: by his merit and his Spirit. Christ's garment of salvation comprises both of these. He communicates his merit to your justification and adoption, and his Spirit to your sanctification. These are great excellencies in Christ's robe of righteousness in his gracious covenant. What a coat of many colors it is; of so many graces for you; are you as excited in it as Joseph was to receive his coat? (Gen. 37:23).

The first thing Christ communicates to the believer is *his merit*, and that, to justification. How is Christ made righteousness to you as a believer? By imputation, by reckoning you as righteous in the sight of God if you believe. It is not only by putting a righteousness into you, but by putting a righteousness over you, even his own righteousness, as a garment. He does this by reckoning to you, his merit, his satisfaction, and his obedience, through this covering garment you are accepted as righteous to eternal life. This is how the righteousness of Christ is communicated to all believers. He is to them, "the Lord their righteousness," (Jeremiah 23:6).

Then, the excellency of Christ can be seen in his continued benefits, all the colors of such a wonderous garment. He adopts you, as his own, where you as a believer are made partakers of the same benefit of divine grace by your engrafting into Christ, your union with him, making you sons and daughters of the most high by grace. "To as many as received him, he gave power, to become the sons of God; even to them that believe on his name," (John 1:12). Christ purchased and procured this benefit for his people and clothes them with it. "When the fullness of time was come, God sent forth his son made of a woman, made under the law, to redeem them that were under the law, that we might receive the adoption of the sons," (Galatians 4:5). And when you believed in him, on your believing, on your receiving of Christ, you were made actual partakers of this benefit as, "heirs of God, and co-heirs with Jesus Christ," (Romans 8:17). There was a time when you were not a son or daughter, and then were. There was a time where you were not clothed with salvation, and then were. You have this benefit from the merit of Christ's work, and are clothed with his garment of salvation that you now have as a believer.

And if you are made a partaker of his merit and work, then, you are made partakers of his Spirit. "Because ye are sons, God hath sent forth the Spirit of his son into your hearts," (Galatians 4:6). This further shows the excellencies of Christ in his benefits of salvation and sanctification, perfecting you throughout your life by this garment of salvation. Christ communicates his Spirit to you as a result of the *benefits* of this spiritual garment that covers you. He does not leave sinners in sin, but has been sent in the great *covenant* of our God to save them from it all.

Yet, this shows further the miserable state of those lost who are not partakers of this grand covenant of grace. If you are lost, you are without a garment. God sees you as naked. Naked people are a reproach to God, and an abomination to him. They are a reproach and abomination because they are left in their sin and nakedness from the fall. And God hates all things related to sin and wickedness in the fall. They are lawless, opposed to his moral character, and have no righteous covering.

Those who willfully stay naked before God are *insane* in doing so. The unregenerate will never desire Christ, even though they are naked. This shows their insanity; it shows how sin makes people insane. They will not put Christ on, they will naturally not be persuaded to cover their shame, or repent, or believe, or turn from their wicked ways. *It is insane to continue to sin before a God who has given Christ so freely, who has given the garments of salvation, and not left men under the curse, but to have life, and that more abundantly. It is insane to desire the naked shame of sin, rather than the giving of Christ and his robe of righteousness in his gracious covenant. To remain naked is to willingly challenge God and look to suffer his wrath.* To be clothed, this is to receive the gift of God giving Christ for lost sinners. Which will a man have?

Christ's righteousness is the righteousness of God for you. It is that righteousness, his garment of salvation, which frees you from the curse of the Law, and covers all your shame, (Heb. 1:8; Rom. 9:5; Matt. 6:33; Rom. 4:6). You should esteem it greatly for it satisfies the wrath of God for you so that you do not have to bear God's wrath. What a power it is to satisfy the angry God. What gift can satisfy the righteousness of God but the righteous robe of Christ's salvation?

You might think to yourself, "well, I do *some* things that are good." Your goodness is imperfect as we discussed before, and hell was created for imperfect creatures. Your works could never justify yourself before God. Your works would have to be perfect, to their fullest extent, and with an infinite righteousness; and so, who is perfect? *You know no one is perfect.* All your righteousnesses are as filthy rags, (Isa. 64:4, 6). The clothes that you have are putrefied and disgusting and so full of sin and holes that they show your nakedness, as if there were nothing to hide you from God's holy gaze. You must cultivate an interest in this Christ, and his robe of righteousness, which God offers to you in the Gospel. It is never something that causes you to merely rest in yourself. It is a righteousness in him that you need. It is not yours; you cannot gain it by buying it, or making it or borrowing it from a friend. It is in Christ, by Christ and through Christ alone. There is no other place to look. The prophet says, "Look unto me, and be ye saved, all the ends of the earth: for I am God, and there is none else," (Isa. 45:22).

You can be fully pardoned by him before God by putting on this garment. All your sins will then not count against you as they do now; many people cannot understand that a Christian's sins don't count against them anymore. People often do not understand how all a person's sins cannot be counted against them in such a free manner. By the obedience of one man (Christ) many are made righteous, (Rom. 5:19); that's how. By his stripes they are healed, (Isa. 53:5); that's how. The blood of Jesus Christ *cleanseth us from all sin*, (1 John 1:7); that's how. And he does this for all sin; yes, all sin, not some, *all*, for this garment is *all* covering, and this covenant is *all* gracious.

"I cannot be saved..." you think. "I cannot believe the Lord Jesus will save me," *many* people have thought. Why? You think, "Because my sins are greater than all other people. I have done terrible things; and in those terrible things they piled up as high as an infinite mountain. My sins are heinous. My sins are against the Gospel. I still continue in my sins even after the Gospel has been preached to me in times past, and preached to me many times; I've sat in many churches, even sung the songs, and tried to pray and took the sacrament." You might think, "I have sinned very often. I have been sinning for a very long time, I'm old in sin. I've not looked to Jesus." Or maybe you are a young person, young in sin, and are so callous at the outset by sin that you run to it freely. You think, "I have secret sins too and willful sins that I love; I don't think I can give them up, and if I can't give them up, I must love them too much, and Christ can never rescue me from such sins. I have even caused other people to sin by my sin." And then you think, "I have no hope of mercy." Now, I'll tell you, thinking that way *is also a sin*, because, as I said before, are your sins so great that Christ could not save you? There is no sin that the all-powerful God could not save you and cause you to rejoice as Isaiah did in the Christ. The Savior's garment of salvation will not only save you, but it will make you *thankful* because it beautifies the wearer. You do have hope, and it is in him alone; but you must gain this garment by having an interest in the Savior. David said, "I was brought low, and he helped me," (Psa. 116:6). You see there, *you have hope,* and *you have help.* God has freely given such a hope and help. He has not left men merely to perish. God is able to *save to the uttermost,* (Heb. 7:25). Christ's righteousness is a robe of salvation that can cover your biggest sins, your longest sins, your smallest sins, *all* of them. Believe on the Lord Jesus Christ and you shall be saved; he promises this!

Consider then, there is Good News for the poor. The good news for the poor, those who are without a garment, those who are naked, Christ freely offers to you a glorious garment ready to put on if you will. You might wonder, "how do I put on Christ? How do I put on this metaphor?" Christ is put on in conversion, and more particularly where God justifies you by faith in his Son because of your belief in him and your turning to him. There you believe in God's only means of salvation. But, you must repent of your sin, for you cannot keep your sins; you can't keep your old clothes. You can't be delivered from your sins and then decide to keep those sins. In the church today a terrible movement started that taught "Lordship Salvation," which is really a new title of an old heresy. It is the Antinomian heresy; *anti* means *against,* and *nomos* means *law,* against the law of God. They teach that you can have Jesus as Savior and not Lord – to do away with his law. How convenient is that? It certainly makes people *feel* very good. You get to keep your sin and have the Savior too! The Antinomian talks this way, "I'm so glad I'm justified by Christ because that's all I need. If I am holy, I am never the better accepted by God; if I am unholy, I am never worse. I'm not looking for graces, but give me Christ; I don't look for graces, I seek for Christ. I may know I am Christ's, not because I crucify the lusts of the flesh, but because I believe Christ has crucified my lusts for me. If Christ is my sanctification, what need do I have to look to anything in myself, to evidence my justification?" You see, they want the Savior without listening to the King. That heresy is militantly destructive to the church, to the professing believer, and is condemned all through scripture, and especially condemned by the words of Christ.[6] For justification, for standing before God, Jesus takes away your sin, so they do not count against you, clothes you with the garment of salvation, covers you in the eyes of God and then fills you with his Holy Spirit so that you can be a worshipper of the Father by faith alone. Then, in this you live for him, and cast off those old clothes, which, in essence, he takes from you. You cannot have those old clothes back; and you cannot live in two suits. In this new robe you live for him. That means what Christ did as a pattern and Savior, you now

---

[6] This is clearly laid out in a longer discussion in my works *Reformation of Heart, Soul and Mind*, and, *The Kingdom of Heaven is Upon You.*

desire to imitate to be conformed into his image; he becomes your hero. People like mimicking their hero. The Spirit in you motions you to be like your hero, your Savior. You can't live like a saint on the Lord's Day and the devil the rest of the week. You have been cleansed by Christ, you cast away your old ways and sin and old life and those garments are taken off, and you put on the new ways of the Christ who has clothed you and you respond with rejoicing and thankfulness. Does that characterize you? Does rejoicing and giving thanks in service to the great King characterize your life?

You who are saints are cautioned in this all through the Scripture. *Don't defile your garment.* A small spot on a white robe is easily seen. Only those who do not defile their garments, will walk with Christ in white, he says. "Thou hast a few names even in Sardis which have not defiled their garments; and they shall walk with me in white: for they are worthy," (Rev. 3:4). This does not mean that what Christ gives you savingly can be permanently defiled and cast off. It does, by way of *metaphor*, though, teach you to cultivate the righteousness that covers you and to wear the robes in such a way that shows forth your appreciation for what Christ has done; to love him back in rejoicing and thankfulness in holy service; clothed with a sure and stable comfort in Christ, yet with a caution and a watchfulness not to defile this gracious covenantal gift he has given you.

In Christ our High Priest we are beautiful and glorious because of his robe. Our beauty is made perfect through his beauty. "...upon thy right hand did stand the queen in gold," (Psalm 45:9). He sees you as *trimmed in gold* as a believer. These glorious robes that Christ has given you ... ...will never wear out. ...will never tear. ... are for all the sons and daughters of the Christ. ... arraying them in incorruption and immortality. ... giving them the privileges and benefits of the Spirit. ... showing them to be heirs of eternity. The rags of sin have been cast away, the apparel of death has been removed, and now you are decked and adorned with beauty and glory, which is the cause of joy, comfort and thankfulness.

Is it not incomprehensible, that as believers you wear the very righteousness of God? The words come out but I can hardly believe the weakness of the statement in human words. You are in a state of justified perfection, though, not the final fullness of that sanctified perfection. You are complete in him, (Col. 2:9-10, 13), though not yet perfect in conformity and conduct as you will be in heaven. But, you are encouraged to think as a believer, "as Christ is, so I am in God's sight, as I am, so Christ is. Whatever is Christ's is mine; what is mine is his; Christ's righteousness is mine. I am all of righteousness; I am as justified by the garment of Christ's salvation as I can ever be. There is no more righteousness that I need to be acquitted by God and seen as righteous, so that he is satisfied with me, than this. I am as righteous and as acceptable *as Christ is* before God. God sees no sin to hinder my justification in me, because there is none in Jesus Christ, for I am covered by this garment of salvation, and there is no spot to be seen." Truly, "Thou art all fair, my love; there is no spot in thee," (Song 4:7). Is not Christ ravished by his spotless bride? "Herein is our love made perfect, that we may have boldness in the day of judgment: because as he is, so are we in this world," (1 John 4:17). In this righteous salvation, this covenant of grace, this garment, there are no spots to be seen as it pertains to being justified before him in Christ.

God has cast all your sins behind his back, (Isa. 38:17). As far as the "East in from the West, so far hath he removed our transgressions from us," (Psa. 103:12). Can you say with the prophet, "I will greatly rejoice in the Lord, my soul shall be joyful in my God, for he hath clothed me with the garments of salvation, he hath covered me with the robe of righteousness," (Isa. 61:10); is that *your* speech? All saints are clothed with Christ's righteousness, for he did not leave men under the curse, but brought forth his Christ *unto salvation* to save you completely and thoroughly. This is what the initial work of the Spirit is in regeneration, conversion, faith and justification; saved to the uttermost in that gracious covenant.

Don't be confused at my saying you have no sin; this is in light of understanding that through Christ one is justified and accounted righteous *in God's eyes.* In Christ *you have no sin,* in that God *counts nothing*

145

against you, you are not condemned if you believe in him and his work. That is an astonishing consideration in light of his law. In the most perfect saints, as you are in yourself, there is remaining sin, but only in regards of your *sanctification*, not your eternal standing before God. "If we say that we have not sinned, we make him a liar, and his word is not in us," (1 John 1:10). But here is the thing, God sees your sin, yet does not condemn you for your sin, because *he has condemned Christ for your sin* if you are a believer. This is why Christ is a *substitute* for those believing. This is where your comfort lies, in that robe that covers you. We say, "...he loved me, and gave himself for me," (Gal. 2:20). Is God not the great Promise Keeper in Christ? Does he not fulfill his covenant *by his only fellow?* What will you do with that notion? What does the prophet say about that notion, and what people who have experienced God's saving hand in Christ in it? "I will greatly rejoice in the LORD, my soul shall be joyful in my God," (Isa. 61:10). What do you believe and think about that righteousness and salvation should be the substance of your rejoicing and thanksgiving (verse 10-11)? That he has done this in the great covenant, certainly! And yet, *how* has he done this?

The fifth principle that we will look at is, knowing that God has not left sinners in Adam's fall, but given them his Christ. In this way God draws you to come to him by the Christ for salvation, making his work very sweet to poor sinners, and continues to draw you closer and closer all your days, which we will look at in the next chapter.

Principle 5:
The Drawing of Sinners to the Lord's Christ

"Ho, every one that thirsteth, come ye to the waters, and he that hath no money; come ye, buy, and eat; yea, come, buy wine and milk without money and without price. Wherefore do ye spend money for that which is not bread? and your labour for that which satisfieth not? hearken diligently unto me, and eat ye that which is good, and let your soul delight itself in fatness. Incline your ear, and come unto me: hear, and your soul shall live; and I will make an everlasting covenant with you, even the sure mercies of David," (Isa. 55:1-3).

In this section of Isaiah, we find God's proclamation, command and invitation to the Gospel. This chapter of Isaiah makes the difference between sincere worshippers of God and hypocrites. There is a difference between those who have wrong motives, and they are those who resist God's plan of salvation. They really have no desire to come to him, to hear him, to grow. They have no real *thirst*. They are not redeeming the preciousness of time. "Seek ye the LORD while he may be found, call ye upon him while he is near," (Isa. 55:6). There is a time when God will not be near, and will not be found. They must call on him, seek him, and they must thirst after him while he can be found. To seek

God, one must be aware of their thirst for him. There would be no need to seek the waters of life if one is not thirsty.[1]

Isaiah 55:1 says, "Ho, every one that thirsteth, come ye to the waters, and he that hath no money; come ye, buy, and eat; yea, come, buy wine and milk without money and without price." The universal call and command that God gives here is to all that are thirsty. It is not specially given to those who are not thirsty, but indiscriminately preached. It is spoken in this way to those that have an *interest*. The interest is based on a need where they are famished; and that there is water that will quench their thirstiness. Literally the prophet says they *come*, or *walk towards life*. The walking, the going to God, the coming to him, is a walking to life and going to life; a coming to life. This exhortation is the good tidings which was promised before by the prophets in the Holy Scriptures many centuries before the Messiah's birth. What follows this exhortation shows that the substance of the command and invitation of the Gospel is limited in effect to "sensible sinners." "Wherefore do ye spend money for that which is not bread? and your labor for that which satisfieth not?" There is an argument for being *sensible* about all this, being *aware* of their thirstiness.

These *thirsty ones* come to the waters that God provides. Like people in the streets hailing others who

---

[1] "I came not to call the righteous, but sinners to repentance," (Luke 5:32).

are marketing their wares, God announces a feast that is open to all those who are thirsty and that desire to come and eat and drink of his Christ. He draws them by the sweetness of the wares, and the superlative excellency of his free gift. In Isaiah 25:6 there is a banquet where God attends sinners, which is referenced by Christ in Matthew 22:8–10 and Luke 14:16–24. In Matthew 22:8 is found the parable of the wedding banquet. Christ tells his servants to bid those on the highways and byways to come and enjoy his feast; his feast is very pleasant, and is free. In Luke 14:16-24 Christ in a parable is the Master who sends his servant out to gather in people for his feast, because those initially who were supposed to come were making very poor excuses to come. "Go out quickly into the streets and lanes of the city, and bring in hither the poor, and the maimed, and the halt, and the blind," (Luke 14:21); in other words, bring those who know their need, those who are *thirsty*.

God then says, verse 2, "Wherefore do ye spend money for that which is not bread? and your labour for that which satisfieth not? hearken diligently unto me, and eat ye that which is good, and let your soul delight itself in fatness." The address is *still* to the thirsty, and God calls attention to excuse makers. Excuse makers spend their money on things of no profit. They spend their own money on things they think will do them good, but will not. It does not satisfy them, or give them their fill. They eat, and yet they are still hungry; they drink, and yet, they are still thirsty. God has something far better because their *spiritual need* is only satiated by God's means.[2] He alone can draw them to places where they can be filled with the water of life. He bids them that he is the only one that can guarantee safety and refuge where the thirsty soul may live. He requires that they listen to him. Obeying God in a way of rightly hearing what he is saying. Hear the summons and partake of the delight of the soul. That which brings goodness, that which is fat. That which is beneficial and pleasant, and that which is of the fatness.

God then says, verse 3, "Incline your ear, and come unto me: hear, and your soul shall live; and I will make an everlasting covenant with you, even the sure mercies of David." God announces that he is setting his invitation and command to come to him within the everlasting covenant that he makes with them showing forth *the sure mercies of David.* God is the reward, God is the gift, God is the feast. Such a feast, gift and reward are all permanent, and such a satisfaction will endure forever. The covenant made with David (*cf.* 2 Sam 7:12–16) who was a type of Christ in this way, was the basis for the church's hope of salvation; unconditional and *sure* (נאמן). "For I will defend this city to save it for mine own sake, and for my servant David's sake," (Isa. 37:35). Such a salvation and a deliverance and an eternal and

---

[2] This is a point the contemporary church should take to heart as it pertains to the means of grace. It is not what they want to do or think they should do (those things which makes them feel so good in their church) that God will improve in them, but only what *God prescribes.* How many churches are deviant in this way alone?

everlasting covenant, the sure mercy of God as it was shown to David and revealed in its fullness in Jesus Christ, is based on a *right hearing.* He tells them, "incline your ear to hear and come. Are you thirsty? Come. Are you hungry? Come. Are you a hearing, thirsty sinner? Come." He is telling the thirsty sinner to come regardless of all else they might be or think they are familiar with in the world which really does not satisfy them in any way. He tells them to not only incline their hear, and walk to him, and come, but to hear, not merely with the ear, but understand what God is commanding, understand what he is offering, and take advantage of it while it can be taken and gained. And, after this, God says, "So shall my word be that goeth forth out of my mouth: it shall not return unto me void, but it shall accomplish that which I please, and it shall prosper in the thing whereto I sent it," (Isa. 55:11). Such a call will be *effectual* for those who thirst.

The fifth principle of the good news is, God calls and draws sinners to himself through Jesus Christ freely. God does not merely give Christ to sinners, but makes all the preparation in drawing in sinners to him, who now may come to him, and *be drawn to him* effectually. He does not give out Christ without giving all the means needed to hear, and come, and eat; he prepares the banquet, and makes it sweet. If they hear, if they come, if they eat, they indeed do all those things because of

God's effectual work in their heart by his Spirit; and then Christ becomes to them their personal Savior.[3]

There are three marks in these verses that show forth God's gracious mercy in drawing sinners to come to him. The first is a general call to all indiscriminately, but a particular call to those who thirst. The second is that they come to buy freely, it costs them nothing to obtain what God commands and offers in his call of salvation. The third is that they are drawn into the covenant of Jesus Christ, given in the everlasting covenant of David which are God's sure mercies to them; and these are superlatively sweet.

[1] Thirsty sinners have been called by God to come to him. The first part of this call is a general indiscriminate call to all, and yet, is also holds in it a particular call to some. There God calls under the sound of the good tidings to come to him, but this call is a command of Christ, to show everyone what their duty is that they must do; surely a *commanding invitation*. And yet, God commands *thirsty sinners* to come to him, which is very particular, "every one that thirsteth, come ye to the waters." All those only who are weary and heavy laden with their sins (Matthew 11:28) who thirst and sensibly feel their need of drink, or who are penitent and feel their misery (Isaiah 61:1), may come and partake of this grand feast. God has promised to give them the water of life which quenches all thirst. The general call

---

[3] See John 3:1-10 and Jesus' teaching on being born again *before* being able to perceive the truth of the Gospel.

of the Gospel has a special call of God, not merely to all men all over the face of the earth, but to *thirsty men,* it is indiscriminate in its sound from the preacher's mouth (all), but discriminate to those the Spirit will call by his power (some).[4] Though it may be indiscriminately said that God calls all those who thirst to himself in a large crowd of people, there is a special call to those that are thirsty. Jesus Christ by his Spirit opens the riches of the Gospel of the grace in him to their souls by his Spirit inwardly and causes them to know their thirst, gives them new palates to taste of his sweetness. He shows this to them in their heart. Others may come and hear the outward call, they might hear that thirsty people ought to come God, but they have no inward desire to come; and they do not know what it means to thirst. They have never journeyed far and long in the valleys and deserts of sin to become thirsty. When a minister of God opens the good news to them, and shows how God has given his Son to them, how he has become incarnate, lived in holiness, died on a cross, was raised from the dead and now is at the right hand of the Father interceding for sinners, the minister says that they are required in this good news to believe it, to believe the sure mercies of David, the everlasting covenant in Jesus Christ to salvation. These people hear his outward call, but that does not mean they are affected by it; it doesn't move their adamant (stony) heart. The riches of God's

---

[4] See my work *The Two Wills of God Made Easy* for a full discussion of this topic.

Christ may be opened to them, but they hear it as with deaf ears; for it is only given to them *outwardly.* They are not moved by it, do not really have an interest in it or in him, for they do not actually see their need of him and thirst.[5]

However, with *thirsty* souls, there is a far different affect that occurs. When the Lord bids thirsty souls to come, when he calls thirsty souls to eat and drink of his feast, there his invitation is *effectual.* He gives those souls an inward call by the Spirit as much as an outward call. They hear that they must have an interest in God's Christ, they must believe on him, they must eat at his table, prepared by God himself, and partake of his feast, and yet, God then comes particularly to that soul and calls them inwardly by the power of his Spirit. There they are sovereignly given a garment of salvation which allows them entrance into the great feast, and they come and dine on Christ's delicacies. As much as there is a physical voice that the preacher uses to preach the word and the good news that men are required to hear, God also preaches to the heart in these Scriptural words, and the Spirit will, in a very particular way, speak to the soul and heart of a person to cause them to truly hear what the message of the good news is, and what it means personally to them and for them. This is where the Spirit of God will so

---

[5] "A new heart also will I give you, and a new spirit will I put within you: and I will take away the stony heart out of your flesh, and I will give you an heart of flesh," (Ezek. 36:26).

work on the heart that the soul is pointed to a certain place in a certain way to the Christ to partake of salvation in him alone; drawn as it were by the Spirit, birth from above (John 3). "Draw me, we will run after thee," (Song of Songs 1:4). The way that soul has gone in times past is not satisfying; they know this because the Spirit has now supernaturally shown them. It is not of *spiritual fatness* they have walked in times past; it is of the lean cows in the Nile. It is not of wine and milk; but bitterness and gall. All the while such a soul is perishing in the wrong way, in a selfish way, and they are not walking, coming, going, to Christ in the right way, but they are now made sensible to it by the Spirit's drawing power so that their thirsty souls may *now* take a drink. The Spirit points all this out to them and gives them all the necessary inclination to enjoy what they hear.[6] As much as there is a general call for all who thirst to come, after this general call, when God sends his Spirit to trouble a soul and make it to thirst after him, when he sees the soul troubled in this way, motioned and moved by the Spirit, the Lord gives a particular call to him, and says, "Ho! everyone that thirsts, you soul, that thirst, come to me, eat of my feast, eat of my table, drink of my Son, eat of the sure mercies of David in my everlasting covenant." Christ never merely says in general, "everyone who thirsts come," but he comes to them in

---

[6] This is called regeneration. "Not by works of righteousness which we have done, but according to his mercy he saved us, by the washing of regeneration, and renewing of the Holy Ghost," (Titus 3:5).

particular, to save them *personally* by his Spirit, and make their heart his throne, and such are then *inclined* to come.

This command and invitation of God through Jesus Christ and his covenant, when it is effectual, has that voice of the Shepherd in it, in an *effectual power* that goes along with it. This is a power that overcomes sin and the fall and changes the heart that it would hear the voice of Christ speaking to them; "for my sheep hear my voice." Christ's invitation is linked to the Spirit's power to make the heart moved to follow the Lord. "And a certain woman named Lydia, a seller of purple, of the city of Thyatira, which worshipped God, heard us: *whose heart the Lord opened,* that she attended unto the things which were spoken of Paul," (Act. 16:14). Such a command and invitation is effectual because it comes with a mighty power to open the heart, a secret virtue that is joined with the voice of the Shepherd that overcomes and conquers the fall in the soul and makes it so new, the person is then regarded as a new man and a new creature, with a new heart that is now *opened* to the truth which is preached. "A new heart also will I give you, and a new spirit will I put within you," (Ezek. 36:26). This is not something God does for all men. When he does it for men, this *new man* then believes that he should come, ought to come, and in no way will be stopped from coming, and will in fact come to the waters to drink and the feast to eat, no matter what.

Such souls then partake of the marrow of the Christ, and eat their fill, and that, into eternity.

When the Lord Jesus in his sure mercies stretches forth his hand to grasp hold of that thirsty sinner, to draw (drag)[7] in the sinner to himself, he sees that reflex act of faith which has been implanted that now springs forth because the Spirit has made that soul, that sinner, hear the call not only with his ears, but with his spiritually persuaded mind and moved in his new heart. Christ reaches for that soul and draws the heart to himself, and so they believe in him. Here the soul finds all those bids of mercy to be sweet, and powerful, and working in them in such a way as they now walk, go, come, to take of that which God had so graciously given them in Christ's covenant. "All that the Father giveth me shall come to me; and him that cometh to me I will in no wise cast out," (John 6:37). The infinite condescension and love of Christ is so clearly seen by thirsty souls, for in his commands and invitations to those souls he calls them to come to him for life, deliverance, mercy, grace, peace, and everlasting salvation; which they will not find in any other, and they now know this. There is only one feast to feast on. Scripture is filled with such commands and invitations to Christ in this way. They are *filled up* with those *blessed encouragements* which God's divine

---

[7] "No man can come to me, except the Father which hath sent me draw him: and I will raise him up at the last day," (John 6:44). The word "draw" is the same word used in Acts 16:19 where, "they caught Paul and Silas, and drew them into the marketplace unto the rulers," *i.e. dragged* them into the marketplace.

provision can apply to lost thirsty sinners who must come to him for rest, even in their present state and condition. God does not require these sinners to climb a high mountain, or work a long work for years to gain some merit before him. They are unable to do so, and they know that too. That in the declaration of these good tidings Jesus Christ stands before sinners, calling, inviting, and encouraging them to come to him and they are to do so freely, wooed (meaning drawn or dragged not merely coaxed) by his Spirit to come to the feast and feed on him.

Thirsty sinners come freely to Christ because they are changed to do so. Consider, God's infinite condescension, grace, and love in his call. He specifically says that souls come to him without money, without price, without barter, without works, without anything. They come to freely eat. They come to freely drink. They come to gain their fill of Christ the Savior, and they look on his sweetness and his excellencies and his wonderful grace freely which takes away their sins. Now it is true, this salvation cost God the life of his dear Son. But this cost Christ was willing to pay to save poor, lost, thirsty sinners. "...for I am not come to call the righteous, but sinners to repentance," (Matt. 9:13).

Why does God call such thirsty sinners to himself? Isn't everything Isaiah said of a free nature to everyone. What does God get out of the deal, so to speak? Why all this tender mercy and everlasting love towards thirsty sinners? Does God stand in need of them? Are they in some way deserving? Did they do something that caught God's eye? Is there anything so special in them that God paused in all his providential work to take notice of a wicked sinner who had rebelled against him? No, nothing at all. God would have been eternally content to leave sinners in their sin. There is nothing in the call of God on the soul, on the heart, other than the flood of overflowing mercy, compassion, and grace, that moves him to act in that way in Christ towards such lost souls. And yet, Christ is very ready to receive such sinners to himself. Christ is ready, where all thirsty sinners should come to him *speedily.* What is there to hinder them from coming? Nothing can truly stop them from coming to God. Can the devil stop them? No. God has cleared the road, so to speak, for them to come. There is nothing to hinder, nothing to stop that soul, nothing set before him while Jesus remains *ready.* The devil will try but fail. The garment of salvation freely given will stop him dead in his tracks. Christ has made provision, and all is ready. Christ calls these sinners to cast their nets again into the sea, at least once more to retrieve the riches of Christ and his glory on *that* side of the boat. There is the miraculous catch of fish waiting. They will find rest for their souls in this. Is there a fear? Is there some anguish or sorrow or pain? Christ is ready to heal that sinner and make them like a new man. He is engaged by covenant to God the Father and will save all thirsty sinners who come to him by the Spirit. He will give them refreshment, abundant life, even his Spirit. At what cost? None to the sinner, it's free in every way. Christ desires to have thirsty sinners come to him and close with him. He desires this, "For the LORD hath chosen Zion; he hath desired it for his habitation," (Psa. 132:13). He desires thirsty sinners to come, to make his habitation with them? Assuredly. "O Jerusalem, Jerusalem, thou that killest the prophets, and stonest them which are sent unto thee, how often would I have gathered thy children together, even as a hen gathereth her chickens under her wings, and ye would not!" (Matt. 23:37). There is no reason why thirsty sinners cannot freely embrace Christ by faith; there are various reasons that the Scriptures give to show that this is the case. Thirsty sinners, worked upon by the Spirit, have *no* recourse to do otherwise. But it is greatly saddening that a soul should spend its whole life searching and buying and purchasing things of the world, the flesh and devil, which profit him nothing, and deceive him, and take him off the path, where Christ has opened up this singular path of eternal life for all thirsty sinners. Why would a soul choose a hard life under the laws of the devil, under worldly care and fleshly desire, where there is an everlasting covenant of sure mercies to be found in Christ Jesus!

If such sinners come freely to Jesus Christ it is a sure sign that God through Christ has loved them from the foundation of the world.[8] Thirsty sinners Christ loves, and loves from all eternity, and died for them, and secures for them the sure mercies of his everlasting covenant. Through Jesus Christ such souls can freely come to God the Father, for he is the way the truth, and the life; he is the door, by which if any man enters, he shall be saved. He requires no money from them, nothing at all; there is no earthly thing that can compare to his precious blood for purchase. If poor sinners have no money, they may come. They are required only to bring their sins to him, which they desire to rid themselves of anyway. Christ sent out his servant to invite the poor, the maimed, the blind, those with sins, to the wedding feast. In this, Jesus Christ should be greatly admired of thirsty sinners, for he is the one who bids them as a thirsty soul to come drink of his waters freely and partake of eternal life freely and does not charge them anything for these things. And, yet, he takes away their sin; whatever harms them most, he removes its condemning power. It cost him his whole life to secure it for them. He is the remedy for all their evil, the source of the free waters that will flow from them for eternal life. John 6:37, "Him that cometh to me, I will in no wise cast out," being so very gracious in this way.

The good tidings are free, and they exhort, plead, prod, summon, invite, command, and call thirsty sinners

---

[8] "According as he hath chosen us in him before the foundation of the world, that we should be holy and without blame before him in love," (Eph. 1:4).

to come to God's Savior. Is there an exception for sinners in this? Does Jesus say all that thirst, let them come to me and drink, except, grumpy sinners, or old sinners, or young sinners, or heinous sinners, or any kind? There are no exceptions in that. Christ desires that sinners merely be thirsty, desire a drink from him, and they can freely come to him. How gracious Christ is here in this passage of Isaiah inviting everyone that thirsts, and he does it by way of repetition. He commands and invites over and over again in this. "Come ye to the waters, come, buy and eat; yes come!" "Come, buy wine and milk!" "Come, he that hath no money, come without money, and without price!" What a pleading in all this, what mercy is this that God would argue sinners into the kingdom in this way? "Wherefore do ye spend money for that which is not bread? and your labor for that which satisfieth not? Hearken diligently unto me, and eat ye that which is good, and let your soul delight itself in fatness." Why do sinners try to earn this salvation *so often?* It is a needless venture for the sinner (the natural man) to continue laboring and sweating and working for that which can never help them, which they can *never* earn. There is no rest to be found by sinners on their own.[9] There is no righteousness that can be worked up and laid at Christ's feet before his throne. No sinner will ever lay anything at Christ's feet on judgment day. They will know it will

---

[9] "Thus saith the LORD; Cursed be the man that trusteth in man, and maketh flesh his arm, and whose heart departeth from the LORD," (Jer. 17:5).

do them no good. They cannot and have not worked anything good, for only Christ's works are good, and meritorious. Jesus Christ has made the provision; and so they will glorify him in that. The thirsty sinner merely needs to lay hold of it by faith. "Incline your ear, and come unto me: Hear, and your soul shall live, and I will make an everlasting covenant with you, even the sure mercies of David." Is this not what Christ says, Matthew 11:28-30, "Come unto me, all ye that labor and are heavy laden, and I will give you rest. Take my yoke upon you, and learn of me, for I am meek and lowly in heart, and ye shall find rest to your souls. For my yoke is easy, and my burden is light." And John exhorts in Revelation 22:16-17, "Come. And let him that heareth say, "Come" and let him that is athirst come. And whosoever will, let him take of the water of life freely."

The Lord Jesus Christ is very desirous that sinners, thirsty sinners, should come to him for relief, that they should be saved, that they should have revitalizing and transforming virtue from him, grace, mercy, peace, and whatever will do their souls good, and that freely given. "Let him that is athirst come," (Revelation 22:17).

[3] Thirsty sinners are drawn into God's covenant by the mercy of Christ. The Covenant of Grace made from eternity is a wonderous truth. The work which Christ fulfilled was *from eternity*. It was a necessary work, and agreement between the Father, Son and Spirit, where God would save these sinners through

the work of Christ from the fall; he will reverse the fall in them, and make them as a bride adorned for her husband. God was under no obligation to save any sinners. It was accomplished freely by God's goodness and grace and pity and mercy in his Christ. When God had decreed and determined to redeem and save thirsty sinners by Jesus Christ; then it became necessary that the decree of God should be fulfilled according to his will. Acts 4:28, "To do whatsoever thy hand, and counsel had before determined to be done." And this agreement between the Father and the Son, Christ says, "Truly the Son of Man goeth as it was determined," (Luke 22:22). He came into the world to do all the Father's will in the power of the Spirit for God's glory first, and for the good of sinners second. As God makes a covenant, an agreement with the Son to save such sinners, so God covenants with men, with sinners to be saved by Jesus Christ. That God would pay such a mind to sinners in this way is a most remarkable thing.

It was a very valuable and costly work to the Father, and to all those who are saved by his work. Christ was obedient to fulfill all the work the Father gave him, he did it freely of his own accord, zealously that no part of any of his work would be left out, and fully, that all God required would be fulfilled. It cost him his life, but he did the work so thoroughly and perfectly that God raised him from the dead and exalted him at the right hand of the throne of God! From there he intercedes on behalf of these sinners, sending his Spirit to give them new hearts, to work in those new hearts, and bestowing on them all the benefits that he procured. All this made his sweet covenant sure, and secure and gives such sinners the blessings of the covenant, the sure mercies of David. "He that spared not his own Son, but delivered him up for us all, how shall he not with him also freely give us all things?" (Rom. 8:32). The mercies of David are all fulfilled in the *spiritual David* Jesus Christ. He is the great prophet, priest and king who saves his people *to the uttermost*. All things pertaining to life and godliness and salvation are given by way of covenant through Christ to those who come to him, to drink of the sweet waters of life freely, to eat of his table, to partake of his fatness and to delight their souls in plenty.

Is this not all based on what the prophet preached? Hear the paraphrase of all this from Isaiah:

Is this not unbelievable? Is it not amazing that God would reveal himself in such a way and manner for the salvation of souls? It is not the way in which men think. He comes forth like a dry stick, with nothing that anyone would take notice of. Even when he came on the scene there was nothing that men saw in his form that was attractive. In fact, they hated him, despised him, and rejected him. A man of sorrows, and acquainted with grief. Men did not even look on him and did not esteem him as the Father's sure mercies. But he suffered as a servant, bearing all the ills of his people, all their sorrows, even to the point of being rejected of the Father, struck by the hand of God, as it were, afflicted for the good of these sinners who thirst for peace. He was nailed to the cross with death wounds for their transgressions, bled out and died there, where the reconciliation of their peace was on him, and he healed them by all the miseries leading up to that cursed death, even by his lashes and stripes, being afflicted in this they are healed. It is very true, all such sinners were like wandering sheep. They have turned away from him, and they have gone astray, walking in paths they thought would have gotten them somewhere, which, in reality only got them quicker on the road to hell. But all their turning, all their going astray, this Lord of mercy has placed on his Christ their sins and punished Christ instead of them. This Jesus did it for the joy set before him, that he would in fact see the travail of his soul, and being oppressed and afflicted, he did it all to the glory of God without complaining, brought, as it were, the sacrifice of the Paschal lamb to the slaughter of God's ordained plan to save thirsty sinners. In this he didn't even open his mouth. He was cut off from the Father's blessing, stricken and set under the great burden of darkness for his people. He died, even though he was innocent, he had done no violence, there was no sin in him. Yet, for such sinners it pleased the LORD to strike him, and put him to grief. He was, given for them, an offering for sin. But he was promised, by the Father, that he would see the travail of his soul, and the pleasure of the LORD shall prosper in his hand. He was satisfied in all this. It is by his knowledge of the way of God that thirsty sinners are justified by him. He bore their iniquities as God's righteous servant. Yes, he poured forth his soul to death, even death of the cross, but was raised up for all these who are drawn to God by such a proclamation. He bore their sin, and made intercession for the transgressors. (see Isaiah 53, the whole chapter).

And what does all this preach but *Kingdom domination* over the fall by the Lord's Christ? Do these truths not bear out the sweetness of the work of the Christ to draw such sinners to himself by his powerful Spirit?

God calls all those who thirst to come to him. Everyone is a sinner, but are you a thirsty sinner? When a sinner is struck with a sense of his sin, and of his necessity of changing his way, amending his ways, reforming his ways, and of his utter inability to do this himself under fear of judgment and damnation, he looks to the Lord and cries out to Christ for his saving hand. Have you done this? God has set his mercy and grace before you in Christ, and shown you what you need to do. He calls you to come to him if you thirst; draws you with cords of mercy and love. Have you come to him freely? God has even placed a number of arguments before you that you should come and not waste your time with things of no profit. The things of the world will *never* satisfy you. God is ready to show mercy in Christ to you, the very sure mercies of the covenant of the Spiritual David. He is so ready to save you that he extends his offer that you may lay hold of Jesus Christ by faith, and amend your lives to live in a way in which glorifies the Son of God.

Is it not a very gracious invitation that he gives you, "Ho, every one that thirsteth, come ye to the waters, and he that hath no money; come ye, buy and eat; yea, come, buy wine and milk, without money and without price," (Isaiah 55:1). He beckons you, "Look unto me, and be ye saved, all the ends of the earth." "Come unto me, all ye that labor and are heavy laden, and I will give you rest." What will you say to him? I'll tell you the answer of the sinner who thirsts after such a sweet feast, "Lord, be merciful to me a sinner," (Luke 18:13). This kind of prayer *shows* your thirst.

Look to Jesus Christ for sure mercy, for he is enough. You think, "But I am such a terrible sinner." Jesus is enough of a Savior. You think, "But I have sinned so long and so hard. Jesus is enough of a Savior to save you." You are not more than a sinner than he can save. You are not a greater sinner than he is a Savior. Cast off that excuse, it will *not help you* when you stand before the judgment seat of Christ to cry out that you were a great sinner and so you threw off God's gracious invitation to be saved. In the work and merit of Jesus Christ, the holy God, there is enough in his obedience, death, resurrection and present intercession to save the worst of sinners. "He is able to save unto the uttermost *all* those that come unto God by him." *All*, yes, every one of them. You come to God to look to him to be saved, and know that Christ is enough, and that he is the sure mercy you seek, that which alone can satisfy your soul; and such things will fill you with everlasting and living waters, and the fullness of a sweet feast.

Christ's very work, the established office of his covenant, is to bring thirsty sinners to God. This is one reason why Christ came as God incarnate, and made reconciliation for sinners like you. Isaiah 53:12 says, "Thou hast received gifts for men, yea, for the rebellious also." Yes, you are rebellious, you rebelled against God and his law. But if you thirst for the waters you can come freely; if you are hungry for righteousness for the feast which he has prepared, then Christ bids you to come and take and eat without money and without price of his dainties. You might think to yourself, "Yes, I have been a very bad sinner. I have been very naughty in every way. Very selfish. Filled with self-love. I have been this way from the womb. Is there no one that can save me?" Christ can save you and receives the rebellious and makes intercession for thirsty sinners. And he will and can do that for you. Tell him what it is you need from him, come and buy at his storehouse of spiritual goods, and he will satisfy you; he has *promised* to do so. He will help you to partake of this great salvation and deliver you from sin and hell, and God's wrath. You will have salvation, deliverance from all fear, anxieties and even death itself. Death itself will have no power over you, and it will lose its sting, for Christ even makes death sweet, for it brings the sinner into his everlasting arms.

Does not Christ himself beckon such sinners, weary sinners to come to him, to be drawn to this holy work for salvation? "I will give you rest," "Ye shall find rest to your souls," "everyone that thirsteth come ye to the waters." Is this what *you* want? Come to Christ, and you will receive rest for your soul, and marrow, and fatness, and feasting. It is interesting to me that God, when bringing the Israelites into the promised land, that he tells them its dripping with milk and honey; *dairy products and sugar.* This is because Christ is *very sweet* in all his work, and filled with fatness in his salvation. It is a sweet rest in him alone, for salvation is very sweet in this way.

And in all this it is interesting, God does not merely sit on his throne in heaven and command you to come, Christ not only calls you from his throne to come, *but he comes to you.* His drawing of sinners is not by distance, but by nearness. He comes to you by his work and death. He came near to you; while you were still a sinner *he comes.* He came to beckon you, to draw near to you, that you would then draw near to him. Thirsty hearts love God's beckoning invitations. He draws you by cords of love as a friend and a Savior. "I drew them with ... bands of love," (Hosea 11:4). What will draw thirsty sinners to come and drink freely but the beauty of Jesus Christ in all his work for precious souls? Do you see his glory clearly in all this? Can you from this very point taste of the sweetness in his work and covenant?

Christ is the fountain, the wellspring, the overflowing waters of salvation. He invites all those who thirst, to come and drink; take a sip, find the sweet sips of Christ in such waters. What kind of drink does he have? He is the only one who has the free, satisfying, and eternal water of life. These are curing waters, quickening waters, for all those who seek comfort and refreshment for their souls. That is why such waters are called "living waters," (John 7:38). It makes those who were dead in sin alive, and such waters make them satisfied in him alone.

You should very well know that nothing can fill the heart of man but God who made man. Will a man really be satisfied with gold and silver and fame and health? What is gold in hell? Ask Jeroboam about his golden calves he made and whether they help him now in hell. What is fame in hell? Ask any celebrity, and famous person who was a Christ-denier in their life, about how they feel about their fame *now*. If you are not filled with Jesus Christ, then you are by necessity filled with the things of hell. Your heart is a storehouse, and what do you store most? The things of the world are fleeting, fading and destructive to you; they will damn you and be bitter to your taste there. Jesus tells you that you must hunger and thirst after that which is righteous and sweet. It is a hunger and thirst after him. It is to find his waters and his table most satisfying; his righteousness that covers the weary sinner and saves them from the wrath of God against sin.

And you may very well deceive yourself into thinking that by some outward show, some outward prayer that you prayed at some point, ushers you into heaven; people have had doubts of their salvation, and what do they do, but pull a card out where they signed on a dotted line on a saving promise or something that a quirky church group gave out rendering some odd idea of assurance. Jesus Christ is not approached by an outward show. If your dry tongue prays a prayer, but your heart is not thirsting after the waters of righteousness, what good is it? Hebrews 11:6, "Without faith it is impossible to please God." Only those that come to Christ by faith, by believing these sweet spiritual truths about him, all that has been discussed in these spiritual principles, will be saved. You must come to God if you desire to please him, for he bids you to come to his waters freely and his table without money and without price. You must look to Christ who is the fountain of all goodness, and know that only those who thirst after him will drink to their eternal satisfaction.

Is it possible for you to come to Christ and be thirsty, yet remain in your sin? Impossible; it is an affront to God to think so. God will never be a sinner's friend and help if the sinner remains an enemy to God and Christ. You must think, "Let my soul bless God forever, for having revealed this great mystery in Christ to me, this covenant, this salvation and Savior, this sure mercy of David, that God may be reconciled to me in Christ, having forgiven me of all my sins by his precious blood. Let me continue in this, feast at his table, and drink of his waters. Let me show this forth in a reformation of my life. Let my new garments of salvation cause me to be distinguished by love for him in sincerity. Let me hold to all spiritual truths, and demonstrate a life that agrees with the word of God. For Jesus Christ, has removed all my sins, covered me with his righteousness and drawn me to him to thirst after him continually, by his Spirit, that I might come to his Father and be embraced by him forever in heaven." Christ will give sinners, who are drawn to him, and thirsty, things of great spiritual satisfaction.

If you are thirsty today, and desire to embrace this great salvation, I invite you to partake of the Christ. All those who thirst for such waters are invited to it. All those who are poor are invited and given it. All those who are weary are motioned to it. All those that are burdened by sin, yes, *thirsty sinners* can have it, and that freely.

Do not allow unbelief to stand in your way to gaining that which will do you eternal good. Do not allow presumption, unbelief or discouragement in your state of sin stop you from hearing the voice of the Shepherd and following him. Do not be unwilling, but willing, and do not fall into the sin of earthlimindedness; to be so fixed on the world that you cannot see Christ clearly; to be such a servant of sin that Christ is a blurred image. Know truly, that there is no more provoking sin than a refusal of salvation, which greatly insults God in this that he has drawn you to, or condescended to come and bring to you. It makes no difference of your age. Either young or old can refuse God's offer, refuse his water, his milk, his wine, his feast, his table, his Son. Heaven and Christ await you, and this is the time where salvation begins, so look to him and be ye saved, "Ho, every one that thirsteth, come ye to the waters, and he that hath no money; come ye, buy, and eat; yea, come, buy wine and milk without money and without price," (Isa. 55:1).

Conclusion

To you who are saints who rest satisfied in the sweetness of Christ's feast, I only say to you consider the doctrines of grace which we have covered in these five chapters. The anacronym of TULIP has been plentifully discussed in these five principles. Did you not see it?

People often think that if one teaches the doctrines of grace, that they must use *theological terms* to teach them. And those who do not understand the *first principles* of the Christian Religion often bock at understanding the doctrines of grace, or telling others that those doctrines are in fact the Gospel of Jesus Christ, which must be believed for salvation. Those kinds of people erroneously believe that such doctrines are *not* the Gospel, and that they can be done without or cast away; "toss them away!" for they think the Gospel is *something clsc*, something *simpler*. But as we have seen in the last five chapters, it is *those very things themselves* that comprise the sum and substance of the Gospel, even found in the Old Testament book of Isaiah. These were not merely notions of, "good tidings." These chapters were teaching you the same *doctrines of grace* that have forever been seen as the *Gospel itself.* We were, and we have been considering these good tidings of God's grace, which is set down in such doctrines of God's precious grace in his one and only Redeemer as the Gospel of Jesus Christ. I will say, *shame* on all those that have ever said the Gospel is *something else;* it is a shame to the ministry of any preacher that thinks so.

All we have studied in this is the Gospel. As much as people don't like to use theological terms to describe the Gospel, yes, TULIP is the Gospel. It is a very good summary of the Gospel. It stands for Total Depravity, Unconditional Election, Limited Atonement, Irresistible Grace, and Perseverance of the Saints. TULIP is the Gospel regardless of *the theological words* commonly used to explain it; whether one is a thirsty sinner, or a thief nailed to a cross. Call them *principles* or call them *doctrines*, or *points,* or *truths*, or *heads* to the substance of all religion; it's all the same. They are all excellent summaries of the Gospel of Jesus Christ, just as John 3:16 is.

[Principle 1] God exists. This we find in the "I" and "U" demonstrated quite clearly. [Principle 2] that God is man's Maker and has made humankind in his image. Which introduces the ideas of the "T" and "U" and the "I" as well as the "P." [Principle 3] ... the bad news that all men have sinned in Adam and are under the curse of God. Which teaches the "T" and parts of the "L." And this even connects parts of the "I" and "U" and "P" in those truths if further explained. [Principle 4] God has not left all sinners to perish under Adam's curse, but has given sinners the righteousness of Jesus Christ as a garment to cover them. This is truly all of them quite extensively, TULIP. For Christ does this, not for all sinners, but thirsty sinners. [Principle 5] God calls and draws thirsty sinners to himself through Jesus Christ freely. You have bound up in God's drawing the "ULIP" based upon the "T." There really is no need, in this work, to go over those letters and theological formulations further than we have (other works have done that successfully enough).[1] The principles, though, stand on their own; they all teach the one and the same thing regardless of how we label them.

And just think, all this talk about the Gospel came from *Isaiah's* good tidings. Shall we study the Gospel, the doctrines of grace? Look to the prophet Isaiah. This Old Testament book is where Jesus looked; for the law and prophets speak about him. "These are the words which I spake unto you, while I was yet with you, that all things must be fulfilled, which were written in the law of Moses, and in the prophets, and in the psalms, concerning me," (Luke 24:44). And it is here where we find these five wonderful scriptural truths that will teach the good news of the Gospel, and the doctrines of God's free grace in Jesus Christ to sinners in it sum and substance:

"O Zion, that bringest good tidings, get thee up into the high mountain; O Jerusalem, that bringest good tidings, lift up thy voice with strength; lift it up, be not afraid; say unto the cities of Judah, Behold your God!" (Isa. 40:9).

---

[1] See Loraine Boettner's work, *The Reformed Doctrine of Predestination* for a full discission on these terms; or any good systematic theology work.

"For thy Maker is thine husband; the LORD of hosts is his name; and thy Redeemer the Holy One of Israel; The God of the whole earth shall he be called," (Isa. 54:5).

Yet, "The earth ... is defiled under the inhabitants thereof; because they have transgressed the laws, changed the ordinance, broken the everlasting covenant. Therefore hath the curse devoured the earth, and they that dwell therein are desolate: therefore the inhabitants of the earth are burned ..." (Isa. 24:5-6).

And then, "I will greatly rejoice in the LORD, my soul shall be joyful in my God; for he hath clothed me with the garments of salvation, he hath covered me with the robe of righteousness, as a bridegroom decketh himself with ornaments, and as a bride adorneth herself with her jewels," (Isa. 61:10).

So, "Ho, every one that thirsteth, come ye to the waters, and he that hath no money; come ye, buy, and eat; yea, come, buy wine and milk without money and without price. Wherefore do ye spend money for that which is not bread? and your labour for that which satisfieth not? hearken diligently unto me, and eat ye that which is good, and let your soul delight itself in fatness. Incline your ear, and come unto me: hear, and your soul shall live; and I will make an everlasting covenant with you, even the sure mercies of David," (Isa. 55:1-3).

There you have the *five principles of the Gospel*, the five doctrines of grace, the five letters of Dort, the sweetness of the marrow and substance of Christ's salvation found in the *Sum of Saving Knowledge* of the Westminster Standards, in the catechisms of the standards, in the *1647 Westminster Confession* itself; the sure mercies of God's everlasting covenant through the Christ freely offered to thirsty sinners by grace.

Other Helpful Books Published by Puritan Publications

Consider Dr. McMahon's *5 Marks* series:

5 Marks of Devotion to God
5 Marks of Biblical Reformation
5 Marks of Biblical Commitment to the Visible Body of Christ
5 Marks of a Biblical Disciple
5 Marks of a Biblical Church
5 Marks of Christian Resolve

Also, consider these newly published works:

A Call to Delaying Sinners by Thomas Doolittle (1632–1707)
A Treatise of the Loves of Christ to His Spouse by Samuel Bolton, D.D. (1606-1654)
Attending the Lord's Table by Henry Tozer (1602-1650)
Faith, Election and the Believer's Assurance by George Gifford (1547-1620)
God is Our Refuge and Our Strength by George Gipps (n.d.)
Remembering Your Creator by Matthew Mead (Meade) (1630-1699)
Resisting the Devil with a Steadfast Faith by George Gifford (1547-1620)
Taking Hold of Eternal Life in Christ by George Gifford (1547-1620)
The Believer's Marriage with Christ by Michael Harrison (1640-1729)
The Doctrine of Man's Future Eternity by John Jackson (1600-1648)
The Victorious Christian Soldier in Christ's Army by Urian Oakes (1631–1681)
Zeal for God's House Quickened by Oliver Bowles B.D. (1574-1664?)

www.ingramcontent.com/pod-product-compliance
Lightning Source LLC
Chambersburg PA
CBHW062105080426
42734CB00012B/2764